A BLUEPRINT
FOR ACHIEVING
PEACE ON **EARTH**

RUSSELL E. HILL

ISBN: 146364731X
ISBN-13: 9781463647315
Library of Congress Control Number: 2011911848

CreateSpace, North Charleston, SC

Content

Introductory Remarks

The whole world's a stage and we humans are all actors in a never-ending saga titled *Life on Earth*. However, there are multiple scripts, all of which are being enacted simultaneously. In fact, almost all actors bring their own script and follow it, even though the result is a cacophony of voices, each making a futile attempt to be heard and noticed. What follows are the musings of yet another playwright attempting to create a script that everyone will want to follow.

The purpose of the new script is to enable all of us, as bit players in the new production of *Life on Earth*, to act out our parts in such a way that the play becomes a well-received, smashing success rather than receiving mixed reviews, as has been the case with the present version. To be sure, even in its current version, there are actors who have managed to stand out and gain notice, at least for the brief moment in time during which the spotlight of the world's attention is on them. Meanwhile, most of us are engaged in mindless banter while we scurry about oblivious to the detriment our contribution has on the play's ability to convey its intent to those who are even paying attention.

Hopefully, these introductory remarks are not so obtuse that they fail to properly set the stage for what follows, which is my attempt to present an insightful script for humanity's enactment of *Life on Earth*. Note that I even changed the title to *A Blueprint for Achieving Peace on Earth*. If you read nothing else, please indulge me the miniscule amount of time it will take you to read the following preface.

Preface

O ne of the things that distinguishes human beings from other life forms that inhabit Earth is their ability to question why life on Earth is what it is and why their combination of mental and physical abilities have enabled them to accomplish far more than any other life form that is known to exist on Earth, or anywhere else, for that matter. At present there are two prevalent theories. The oldest and most prevalent is that some unknown, all-powerful entity created everything that exists on Earth and set up all the intricate interactions that were required to enable the original life forms placed on Earth to evolve from their prehistoric versions into the versions that exist today. In fact, most theories in this category assume life on Earth began with humans already pretty much in their present form and with all their thinking and communication capabilities already in place. All they were required to do was to share the bounty that Earth provided them and get along peacefully with one another. Unfortunately, getting along peacefully with one another wasn't that easy to accomplish because, as it turns out, humans are inclined to put their personal needs and desires first, and this inclination inevitably creates conflicts with other humans who are trying to do the same thing.

Furthermore, as humans began to take notice of the way things were, they realized that their abilities were superior to those of the other creatures they encountered. They also recognized that they were at the mercy of natural phenomena that threatened their well-being. Therefore, they attributed storms, volcanic eruptions, earthquakes, failed crops, plagues, and other events that caused death or suffering to whoever had created Earth and them, and they surmised that these kinds of events were this creator's way of expressing displeasure with their behavior. And yet, since humans believed themselves to be smarter than any other creature on Earth, they concluded that Earth and its bounty must have been created for them to use in any way they pleased.

As humans initially developed and propagated, younger generations began to migrate from their place of origin to different places on the Earth in search of land that offered adequate food, water, and shelter. As a result, humans settled in areas that differed from the place where they originated. Over time, as this migration cycle repeated itself, origins were forgotten and geographical features became barriers that prevented migrating groups from easily maintaining contact with one another. Consequently, these isolated groups began to develop dissimilar physical traits as they adapted to each new living environment. In addition, they began to develop language and behavioral traits that differed from other isolated groups.

Since these events occurred before there was any record keeping, physical barriers prevented these isolated groups from remaining aware of their historical connections to other groups. Thus, isolated groups developed independent stories to explain how they originated. They also developed unique rituals that they used to demonstrate their appreciation and homage to the unknown entity they believed had caused it all to happen. Since there was no consistency in appearance, lifestyle, or spiritual beliefs, when one isolated group of human beings encountered another group of human beings, obvious dissimilarities inevitably resulted in conflict.

When conflicts did occur, the group with superior skills, better weapons, or smarter leaders usually prevailed, but inevitably, the winners attributed their success to the superior abilities that they believed had been given them by the entity or entities they believed responsible for their creation and protection. The winners also believed they were entitled to disperse, enslave, or kill the losers to prevent the losers' appearance, beliefs, and lifestyle from contaminating their own physical characteristics and social mores.

Unfortunately, this kind of attitude persists to this day. There are still humans on Earth who believe that killing or abusing other humans is an acceptable solution to eliminating a perceived threat to their social homogeneity, particularly when the victims are distinguishable from themselves in some way thought to be significant enough to justify such actions. This attitude of entitlement has caused some humans to be oblivious to the possibility that the consequence of their behavior is harm to themselves or their descendants or some aspect of Earth's ecology essential to their survival. This is particularly true when the motivation behind their behavior is satisfaction of a need or desire. In other words, humans have tended to focus on the immediacy of the benefit derived from their actions and have tended to ignore the possibility that the ultimate consequence of their actions might be a chain of events that could adversely affect their own existence, adversely impact the existence of other life forms, or impair some aspect of Earth's ability to provide the environment upon which they and Earth's other life forms depend.

This self-centered mind-set has been creating serious problems throughout humanity's existence, but occasionally leaders come along and try to introduce rules for behavior that will enable the individuals within their groups to strike a balance between each person's personal agenda and what is best for all members of the group. Usually, the rules made by the leader of each group are enforced by that leader, who punishes any member of the group who violates the rules. The problem, of course, is that each group's rules for behavior only apply to how members of that group treat one another. They do not necessarily apply to how members of one group treat people who are members of another group. Conflicts between disparate groups are still common, and life continues to be problematic in such instances, but as time has passed, wiser minds have tried to persuade others within their group to adopt a more conciliatory approach in their dealings with members of another group. In such cases, they've introduced inducements that are powerful enough to accomplish that objective. One such approach has been to introduce the revelation that an unseen Supreme Being created Earth and everything on it and is responsible for all that has happened and will happen on Earth. These messengers allege that this Supreme Being has given them a code of conduct that, in fact, the wiser minds developed on their own.

In addition, these so-called messengers have usually claimed that the Supreme Being they've created promised to grant a pleasant afterlife to those who adhere to the prescribed rules throughout their lifetime, but have also warned that those who don't follow the prescribed rules will spend their afterlife in very unpleasant circumstances. As a result, there are multiple groups on Earth whose members have accepted one of these stories, willingly acquiesced to the prescribed rules for behavior, and begun peacefully coexisting with others who choose to buy in to the same belief system. Unfortunately, there is little congruity in the message these selected messengers have delivered. As a result, adherents to the teachings of the various messengers have been disinclined to tolerate anyone whose beliefs differ from theirs.

In other words, the introduction of religion to induce peaceful coexistence has only been successful within the groups of individuals who adhere to the tenets of the same religion, for example, Christians, Muslims, or Hindus. But even within these religious groups, there are sects or denominations whose followers are intolerant of those who choose to engage in different practices of the same faith. As a result, attempts to introduce incentives for peaceful coexistence have often created just another excuse for humans to abuse one another.

So what are the alternatives? Over time, a growing number of people have begun to believe that there is no creator, because, so far, no one has found indisputable evidence that Earth and the rest of the universe were intentionally created. In fact, no one has discovered how all that we know to exist actually came to exist. Nevertheless, we do exist, and the best way for our species to continue its existence is for all human beings on Earth to willingly live peacefully with their neighbors and to continue procreating because both are essential if humanity is going to remain viable on Earth.

At the same time, it is incumbent on every individual to realize that another evolutionary dynamic that is essential to humanity's societal success is the ability to live peacefully with one another. Since the ability to interact with others begins to develop shortly after birth, those responsible for influencing the outcome of this development must be made to understand how important it is for them to provide the kind of nurturing that will help each child in their care become adept at dealing with others equitably. This approach will enable all new human beings to develop into individuals who are capable of embracing every other human being as an esteemed member of their extended family who deserves to be treated with the same care and respect as they are expected to give to members of their own family, to their friends, and to their acquaintances. The evolution of humanity into a uniform society in which every human being has equal standing depends on the development of such an attitude.

In other words, in order for the human species to evolve to the point where all individuals are considered to be members of the same community regardless of where on Earth they happen to live, humans everywhere must learn to engage only in behavior that allows that to happen. That requires people to understand how their behavior affects nature and the development of our species' next generation. Furthermore, this understanding is more essential now than ever before because humanity's technological evolution is creating societal interactions that increase the rate at which Earth's living environment is changing.

Perhaps as our abilities to examine the universe improve, our understanding of how the universe began will improve, and perhaps we will discover other planets that are similar enough to Earth to support human life. These are areas of investigation worthy of pursuit, but as of today, the simple reality is that Earth is the only planet we know of where life as we know it can exist. Therefore, it's time for all humans to accept that unless all humans learn how to peacefully co-exist with one another and how to preserve Earth's ability to sustain our species, some future generation of each of our personal lineages will face extinction.

Humanity must figure out how to overcome its attitudes of entitlement, get along with one another peacefully, and utilize Earth's resources and the things we make from those resources in ways that prolong Earth's ability to support us for as long as possible. No Supreme Being is going to do that for us, so let's stop wasting time and energy arguing about whose version of our and Earth's origin is right or which code of behavior is best. We're here, and it's up to all of us to make things work so the Earth that our future generations inherit from us will be able to support them as effectively as it has supported us and all past generations. Surely, we humans can agree on a code for behavior that enables us to do that.

What follows is divided into two parts. Part 1 discusses various aspects of human nature and how the way human societies have evolved has affected their ability to remain viable on Earth. It then presents suggestions for modifications in behavioral attitudes and ways of accomplishing the tasks that are more likely to achieve the most constructive outcome for humans and for the living environment on which all humans depend.

Part 2 delves into specific changes in the way people accomplish the various aspects of maintaining personal well-being and the societal changes that are required to ensure that all human beings are given every opportunity to manifest any contribution they may be able to make toward improving humanity's ability to remain a viable species on Earth. There are also chapters devoted to ways humans can improve the quality of existence for all members of their species. Each chapter proposes specific changes in behavior to avoid shortening individual lives or shortening the length of time Earth will be able to provide the living conditions necessary to sustain humanity.

PART I
Human Behavioral Traits that Impede Development of a World Community

SECTION 1
Impediments to Establishing Peace on Earth

Based on what is known from research into our history, it is obvious that our existence is the result of an indomitable life force that drives all Earth-bound creatures to propagate to prolong their species' existence on Earth. This is the process that Charles Darwin labeled *natural selection,* and it has enabled all Earth's species that presently exist to continue their existence by developing physical characteristics that enable them to acclimate to Earth's ever-changing living conditions. However, based on fossil evidence, we also know that some species that existed sometime in the past were unable to acclimate to all the changes that occurred during their existence, and they became extinct. These fossil remains should be a reminder to us humans that we too could be on the brink of extinction as Earth's living conditions continue to change and our own behavior influences the nature of those changes.

So far, because of the unique abilities we've developed, our species has been one of the most successful in adapting to changes in Earth's living conditions and in using Earth's resources to thrive. On the other hand, this drive to thrive has not been without consequences, and we are beginning to realize that the lifestyles we've developed are adversely affecting Earth's ability to support us. The following chapters address the attitudes that motivate the kinds of human behavior detrimental to the quality of our own species' existence and to Earth's ability to support us.

CHAPTER 1

Humanity's Attitude of Entitlement

The root cause of humanity's existential predicament is its attitude of entitlement. All animals are instinctively self-interested, and human beings are no different. Their self-interest is the motivating influence driving their attitude of entitlement, which developed early on, when people were primarily concerned with doing whatever they had to do to survive.

Since their attitude of entitlement engenders a lack of concern for the adverse environmental consequences their behavior may cause, humans have a tendency to invent tools and practices that make their lives easier and more enjoyable. In other words, most inventors have focused on attaining the desired result without concerning themselves with the undesirable consequences their inventions might have. Historically, there have been two motivations for invention. First, inventors are driven to create something or introduce a new way of solving a problem that leads to a more satisfactory or pleasing result. Second, inventors may also be motivated by the potential for profit or other benefits that their invention may bring them.

Take chlorofluorocarbons, or CFCs, as an example. These compounds were invented to be used in the production of air-conditioning refrigerants, solvents, foam insulation, and aerosol propellants. Eventually, it became apparent that CFCs do not break down in the atmosphere. Instead, they migrate into the stratosphere, where they destroy the ozone layer that shields Earth's surface from excessive ultraviolet radiation. The problem is, when too much ultraviolet radiation from the Sun reaches Earth's surface, it causes incidences of skin cancer to increase.

A similar kind of problem is caused by polychlorinated biphenyls, or PCBs. PCBs were invented to be used in lubricants, hydraulic fluids, paints, and adhesives. They were also used in coatings for paper and as an additive to make plastics pliable. After an extended period of use, it became apparent that when PCBs find their way into an ecosystem, they poison wildlife and cause cancer in humans. The same is true for the exhaust from internal combustion engines and from the emissions produced by various industrial processes, not to mention the gases produced by fire, decaying matter, and animal flatulence.

Until recently, humans assumed that the atmosphere would absorb all these gases with little ill effect. However, as the volume of gases being produced has increased and Earth's capacity to absorb these gases has decreased, the accumulation in the atmosphere is magnifying the normal greenhouse effect that moderates Earth's temperatures. As a result, Earth's climate has become warmer on average. If this situation is allowed to continue, temperatures will eventually reach levels that make human life on Earth impossible.

One of the reasons Earth's ability to absorb greenhouse gases is decreasing is that land is being cleared of trees and other plants so it can be put to other uses. Since trees and other green plants are one of the most effective ways Earth has for removing greenhouse gases from the atmosphere, a reduction in the number of these plants reduces Earth's capacity for controlling the amount of greenhouse gas in the atmosphere. While some replacement planting does take place, most land that once helped Earth regulate the amount of greenhouse gas in the atmosphere is now being used for purposes that increase the production of greenhouse gases.

Oceans are also effective in removing greenhouse gases from the atmosphere, and some sea creatures use these gases to make the shells they use to protect themselves from predators. This shell-making process takes these greenhouse gases out of circulation indefinitely. However, as higher temperatures warm the water and runoff from industrial and agricultural operations pollute the water, the populations of oceanic organisms that convert these gases into seashells is decreasing and the capacity for absorbing greenhouse gases by the ocean is being diminished. In addition, when too much carbon dioxide is absorbed into the oceans, the water becomes too acidic, which poses additional threats to the well-being of the sea creatures upon which human existence depends.

Furthermore, a lot of the things humans do in pursuit of their own satisfaction end up adversely affecting themselves and others. Smoking cigarettes, taking drugs, consuming excessive amounts of alcoholic beverages, having unprotected sex, or driving while under the influence of anything that impairs motor skills are all examples of things humans do that adversely affect their own well-being and threaten the well-being of innocent bystanders.

This is old news, and those problems are being addressed, but how can we be sure that the inventors of the next great inventions will have done their due diligence to ensure that the products produced and the associated production process does not adversely affect the environment in some way? We can't until we, the people, refuse to accept the use of any procedure or activity that threatens humanity's well-being or Earth's ability to support us. We must all learn to be diligent in ensuring that all aspects of the processes and behavior in which each and every one of us engage, as we strive to attain the lifestyle we desire, are as compatible with Earth's ecosystems as possible. We must also learn to share Earth and its natural resources in a way that ensures the future viability of the human species by teaching humans to focus less on satisfying their own needs and desires and more on taking the needs and desires of others into consideration.

Because our attitude of entitlement is so engrained in the human mindset, very little in the existing body of law controls individual and group actions taken at the expense of what is best for our species and for creation on Earth. It's time for all Earth's citizens to become more consistent in their demands regarding how Earth's resources are converted into useful products and the way those products convert resources into energy. The objective must be to accomplish necessary tasks in the way that does the least harm to Earth and its living environment.

Humanity's attitude of entitlement has also influenced the way land is owned and used. Today, most land on Earth is owned by those whose ancestors initially staked claim to it, or it is owned by the latest in an unbroken chain of acquirers and their beneficiaries. In either case, the largest share of benefits derived from harvesting the resources that a plot of land can produce goes to whoever controls that plot. Benefits also flow to those persons who own the rights to harvest the resources, run the industrial complex that transforms those resources into useful products, market the finished products, and provide the services that support the harvesting, manufacturing, and marketing processes.

This arrangement leaves out a large portion of Earth's population because many people don't own land or the land they do own produces insufficient resources to provide a living and they reside in places where the economic infrastructure does not provide jobs that allow them to earn enough to purchase what they need to sustain themselves in a viable existence. These circumstances cause people, particularly babies, to starve and die of malnutrition or from diseases that they are unable to ward off due to their weakened physical state of being. And even if a baby does survive these circumstances, its vitality is likely to have been curtailed, and that's not right. Earth and its resources should belong to everyone, and all land and its resources should be allocated in a way that enables all human beings to obtain what they need to be viable members of the human species.

Today, those who control the land are not willing to relinquish their control, and they are able to use their influence to ensure that the laws pertaining to land ownership are not changed. As a result, no governmental entity has the power to change the way land is owned or the way its resources are distributed, and that will continue to be the case until the majority of human beings agree that all Earth's resources and the produce of those resources must be shared in a way that enables everyone to support themselves adequately.

In order for this objective to become reality, all human beings must eliminate their attitude of entitlement regarding the use of Earth's land and its resources to create their desired lifestyles. In other words, they must replace their attitude of entitlement with an attitude of responsibility and commitment. To do that, everyone must be willing to correct the mistakes of the past and start doing what's best for all inhabitants of Earth. The challenge is finding a way to convince all human beings that this change in attitude will ultimately lead to a better outcome for everyone.

CHAPTER 2
Manifestations of Humanity's Attitude of Entitlement

Humanity's attitude of entitlement has resulted in an arrogant disregard for how humans' actions affect their own well-being as well as that of other species and Earth's ecosystems. Consider such endeavors as farming, mining, and ranching. Since the effectiveness of these endeavors relies on mechanization, process enhancement, or the use of growth stimulation methods to increase production, failure to anticipate the harmful side effects of new methods has produced undesirable consequences. In farming, land has become less productive because repeated plowings have contributed to soil erosion and repeated applications of chemicals have killed off the microorganisms that make the soil viable for growing things. In mining, strip mining and the pollution created from tailings have rendered the affected land and water resources toxic. In ranching, over grazing has led to soil erosion, and the use of animal growth enhancers has raised questions about food contamination.

Today, humans depend on oil and natural gas as their primary sources of energy production, but energy produced from refined oil products and from natural gas is not renewable. Once gasoline is consumed, the energy source is gone. The only way to replenish that kind of fuel is to pump more oil out of the ground and refine it. The same is true for underground deposits of natural gas.

On the other hand, the energy-producing element in natural gas is also continuously produced by decomposition of organic matter in oxygen-deprived environments and by the digestive processes of most animals. In other words, the organic residue of human lifestyles is a renewable source of energy-producing gas. Today, most of the gas being produced in this manner escapes into the atmosphere where it contributes to global warming.

The point is this: underground deposits of oil and natural gas will eventually be completely depleted and alternatives will have to be developed in order for humanity to continue its reliance on hydrocarbons to power mechanical devices. The best alternative is to capture the methane gas being constantly produced by natural processes and use it as a source of energy instead of allowing it to become a contributing factor in global warming. Therefore, when biodegradable garbage is discarded it should be done systematically so the beneficial byproducts derived from decomposition can be captured and used to produce energy or other products instead of being allowed to decompose in ways that adversely affect some aspect of Earth's environmental balance.

Similarly, clothing should never be thrown away. It should be turned in if the owner has tired of using it and exchanged for a replacement. Turned-in items should be refurbished and made available for exchange unless they are too worn to be refurbished. Then they should be recycled so the recyclable materials can be used for other purposes.

The same is true of other types of durable products. They should not be discarded if they break or because the product is not reusable after it has been used for its initial purpose. If it's broken, it should be fixed and used until it wears out, then it should be turned in so the materials can be recycled and reused. If the product is durable but not reusable after its initial use, for example a food container, it should be turned in so it can be recycled and made into something else.

Manufacturers of durable products should want to create the most durable and long-lasting products possible instead of products that lose their effectiveness in a short time and force users to buy replacements. They should also avoid the practice of creating artificial obsolescence by introducing new designs that tempt consumers to abandon serviceable products in favor of products that perform the same function but produce a more appealing impression. Every product should be designed to use interchangeable parts so only parts that fail need be replaced. That will enable all products to be used until use is no longer environmentally, economically, and operationally prudent.

Of course, these changes will only take place when people change their attitudes regarding the things they acquire and use in the course of living their lives. First, if people have the means, they typically replace the items they use for clothing, conveyance, and entertainment long before the end of each item's useful life. The same is true for items used in preparation of food and maintenance of land and dwelling. Second, if people can afford something, they prefer to acquire it new, rather than used, and they tend to discard used items rather than recycle them. Third, people who acquire things prefer that those things imply status; consequently, the amount of natural resources used to affect the desired image usually results in using more than is necessary.

Conclusion: a lot of people have developed a mind-set that puts satisfaction of their personal agenda ahead of caring about the effect the resulting behavior may have on other humans, on some aspect of creation on Earth, or on the length of time that Earth will be able to sustain acceptable living conditions. The problem with that way of thinking is pretty obvious. Creation is forever, but individual humans and the species as a whole have a finite life expectancy. On the other hand, the length and quality of that lifetime are determined by the choices each individual human makes. If humans learn to control those actions that lead to a disruption in the natural balance of their own physiology, and they learn to curtail those actions that disrupt the natural balance in creation, individual lives will be longer, healthier, and more enjoyable, and the life span of the human species on Earth will be extended.

The bottom line is that we have got to do a better job of anticipating how our behavior will impact creation's ability to sustain a livable environment on Earth and avoid engaging in any behavior and activities that cause some aspect of creation on Earth to malfunction. If we don't, our species will eventually reach the point at which our survival is no longer possible.

CHAPTER 3

Harmful Aspects of Human Behavior Motivated by Ego

The human ego is what motivates human behavior when self-esteem or self-importance is at stake. It's a byproduct of the innate will to live and the need to succeed in every undertaking. In humans, it's more than accomplishing whatever is necessary to survive and satisfy one's physical needs. It involves doing whatever is necessary to establish the desired persona. The following is an attempt to identify those aspects of human behavior that are influenced by ego.

SUSCEPTIBILITY TO INCITEMENT

Because of the innate will to live and the need to succeed in every undertaking, when an individual or group fails to attain a desired result, hate, rage, envy, jealousy, and resentment are likely to ensue, particularly if the individual or group that has failed believes the failure is due to circumstances contrived by others to prevent success. People often act on what they've been led to believe is true, whether it is or not. One person with an agenda can influence others to act a certain way by creating the perception that a wrong has occurred or might occur unless actions are taken to prevent it from happening. That's how wars, race riots, and hate crimes are instigated.

DELUSIONS OF SUPERIORITY

Humans tend to discount the lives of anyone whose appearance or lifestyle is considered a threat to their perceived superiority. As a result, exclusionary actions are taken to isolate those who are considered to be a threat. In some cases, more extreme measures are taken. Hundreds of thousands of individuals die prematurely every year because they encounter someone who perceives them to be a threat to their own way of life. In fact, it's not unusual for humans to consider murder when attempting to protect themselves from the threat that they perceive others represent.

In some cultures, parents have been known to kill their first child if the child is female because a male child is essential to guarantee the well-being of the parents. Ensuring that the first child is a male guarantees that whatever property the family owns will remain in the family and can be used to support the parents as well as the next generation. Plus the male child is counted on to take care of the parents in their old age. In such cultures, a female takes part of her family's wealth with her as a dowry when she marries, and her allegiance shifts to the family of the man she marries. Because a female's dowry reduces their wealth, it adversely affects the well-being of her parents. In addition, she will not be available to take care of them in their old age.

In other cultures, humans consider it acceptable to mistreat other humans if the humans being mistreated are engaged in a lifestyle that involves acts or practices that deviate from the acts and practices considered acceptable by the majority. In such instances, this kind of mistreatment often results in the death of those who are caught engaging in so-called deviant behavior.

So why do these attitudes have to be changed? The answer is that no one should be intentionally killed for any reason, because from the point of view of species survival, all human beings are precious.

EXPEDIENCY

For most of their existence, humans have focused on attaining a desired result without concerning themselves with whether that result will have undesirable consequences for themselves and for some other aspect of creation on Earth. Typically, people fail to consider all the ramifications that a contemplated action may have before they act and act only if the anticipated result will be, at worst, neutral and at best, beneficial for everyone and everything affected by the action being contemplated.

Some may argue that if our predecessors had been more concerned about the adverse ramifications of their actions when they were developing and implementing the technology associated with the industrial revolution, humanity wouldn't be nearly as advanced as it is today. The thing that has enabled humans to be as successful as they have been is their ability to increase their knowledge by trying new things, and there's nothing wrong with that. People are always on the lookout for ways to make their lives easier and more enjoyable. However, people tend to let their attitude of entitlement be the primary motivation driving their efforts. Anticipated benefits of an invention cause the inventor and users to give little or no thought to the adverse side effects a contemplated invention might have. In fact, until recently, humanity's attitude of entitlement has pretty well obfuscated concern regarding unanticipated consequences.

INVENTIVENESS

The thing that has enabled human beings to successfully inhabit and thrive almost everywhere on Earth is their ability to solve whatever problems impede them from accomplishing the desired objective, whether it is being able to live in extreme weather conditions comfortably or getting from starting point to objective as quickly as possible. Human beings have always sought ways to make life easier and more enjoyable, and there's nothing wrong with that as long as the inventions they embrace do not threaten the well-being of some, if not all, human beings. In other words, the anticipated benefits of a new invention must not cause the inventor or the users of that invention to ignore the possibility that the product's production and use may produce residues or cause damage that adversely affects some aspect of creation on Earth. Instead, inventors must focus on ways of solving problems that do not cause any harm to any aspect of the ecological systems essential for supporting life on Earth. In addition, users of products must insist that the manufacture and use of those products create as little pollution as possible, and that the materials used in their manufacture be recycled when a product's usefulness has been exhausted.

Inventors need to begin considering all the ramifications of a contemplated invention before they introduce it for public consumption. Thomas Edison is a good example of someone with the mental capability to invent practical applications that used electricity to improve the quality of peoples' lives. Ever since, other inventors have continued to conceive new ways to utilize electricity in increasingly sophisticated applications.

Ways to utilize electricity is only one example of how a single invention can initiate a cascade of other inventions. There have also been and continue to be ongoing cascades of inventions that improve the effectiveness and efficiency of tools people have invented to accomplish every kind of human activity more effectively. It began with the simple tools that prehistoric people used to make it easier to obtain their sustenance and to protect themselves from the elements as well as predators. Ways to transport themselves from place to place soon followed. Then, as less time and energy were needed to defend, feed, clothe, shelter, and transport themselves, people began think up various pastimes to occupy themselves during the resulting freed-up time. Naturally, each pastime initiated its own cascade of invention as people thought of ways to improve the accoutrements needed to participate.

The focus of all these inventions has been, for the most part, on making some aspect of daily living easier and more enjoyable. As tools and the other accoutrements of living became more sophisticated, little attention was paid to how the manufacture and use of all these products would affect Earth's ability to sustain life. Now scientists are beginning to realize that there are limits to Earth's resources and to the amount of pollution Earth can absorb without degrading its ability to provide an adequate living environment. Consequently, humanity must accept that present lifestyles will have to change in order to preserve our planet's ability to provide an adequate living environment.

Today, most inventors and consumers are beginning to be more deliberate in considering the effect on Earth's environment and its organisms that contemplated products may have and are eliminating those products and procedures that are known to have undesirable side effects. But the Earth will not be a completely healthy place to live until everyone commits to eliminating all behavior and procedures that adversely affect Earth's ability to support human life.

COMPETITIVENESS

Humanity has been a successful species because humans compete in any situation where self-interest and ego are at stake. Competition is a byproduct of humanity's innate will to live and its need for gratification in all that humans do. It is the inclination to do whatever is necessary to attain the desired result, but in humans, competitiveness can go beyond doing what's necessary to survive and satisfy one's physical needs. It includes doing whatever's necessary to establish the desired persona. In that sense, competition is also a means by which the human ego is nurtured.

Followers of Buddha have long understood that ego must be replaced with compassion for all of creation if genuine happiness is to be achieved. They understand that as long as humans allow their egos to dictate their behavior, there is little likelihood that they will be able to develop a community in which everyone is allowed to pursue endeavors that best suit their interests and capabilities and enable them to realize happiness and fulfillment without causing harm to anything or anyone else. When competition is ego driven rather than motivated by the enjoyment of participation, the results can be destructive rather than constructive.

Take creative expression for example. Some people are so stimulated by what they observe, envision, or feel that they are compelled to create something that conveys their inspiration to others. This is the process that individuals use to affect the thinking, feelings, and actions of others. On the other hand, the ego can be manipulated by anyone with an agenda, and that's a good example of how creativity can be used destructively. Fortunately, individuals occasionally introduce an idea or concept that leads to an improvement in the human condition, and that's a good example of how creativity can be used constructively.

To be successful in competitive situations requires creativity and ingenuity as well as physical skill and determination. In competitive situations, those who are the most skillful, ingenious, creative, and determined usually prevail, but our competitive nature also motivates those who have been bested in a competitive situation to resolve to do whatever they can to change the results. When their motive is to simply improve their abilities so that the next competition may have a more favorable result, competition is healthy, but when they resolve to avoid losing by cheating, it's not.

In a debate, the objective is to sort out the best course of action in attaining a desired objective. In such instances, the debating parties must feel free to express their points of view, knowing full well that they are trying to influence those with an opposing viewpoint to change their minds. There's nothing wrong with that as long as both parties present their argument in an honest, straightforward manner and willingly accept the solution deemed best by the majority of those affected by the course of action being debated. But when people intentionally use half-truths and innuendo to try to win, they are no longer competing fairly.

SEXUALITY

Sexual intercourse is nature's way of ensuring a species' survival. However, when sexual arousal occurs but other circumstances make it imprudent to pursue intercourse, such impulses must be suppressed because doing so will circumvent the harmful effect that satisfying such impulses may ultimately have on the participants or on others who are intimately related to the participants. After all, the whole objective of sex is to bring two people together to experience all the aspects of living that create happiness and satisfaction from sustaining and nurturing one another to creating, sustaining, and nurturing offspring.

Incest, rape, adultery, and unprotected intercourse can be hurtful to one or all parties involved. Therefore, it is important for unattached individuals to avoid having intercourse simply to satisfy their sexual appetites, because sexual intercourse between two humans is completely satisfying only when both participants get back as much as they give, and that rarely happens in casual sex. In fact, the more likely outcome is that one or both of the participants will end up feeling unfulfilled or worse, used, in which case, instead of being the catalyst that transforms a relationship into a long-lasting, fulfilling experience, sexual intercourse becomes a detrimental influence that threatens to undermine the relationship.

Sex is like a narcotic. People get addicted and lose perspective. Having sex just to satisfy one's physical needs is an impediment to a fulfilling relationship and this kind of sexual intercourse is likely to be demeaning for one, if not both, participants. There is a vast difference between admiring the physical attractiveness of an individual and desiring physical intercourse with that person. Therefore, all persons should learn to appreciate the beauty in the person beheld without considering that person to be a candidate for sexual conquest.

On the other hand, there's nothing wrong with self-stimulation as long as it doesn't adversely affect anyone else. Masturbation is a way to relieve sexual tension when intercourse is not a prudent option. The problem is that self-stimulation can rob a relationship of its spontaneity, and spontaneity is one of the most wonderful aspects of a couple's sexual interaction. Worse yet, self-stimulation may affect one partner's willingness to respond to the needs of the other, and that can have a negative impact on one of the most fulfilling aspects of an intimate relationship.

LAND OWNERSHIP AND USE

Today, most land on Earth is owned by those whose ancestors initially staked claim to it, or it is owned by the latest in an unbroken chain of acquirers and their beneficiaries. In either case, the largest share of benefits derived from harvesting the resources that a plot of land can produce goes to whoever controls that plot. Benefits also flow to those persons who own the rights to harvest the resources, to the owners and managers of the industrial complex that transforms those resources into useful products, to those who market the finished products, and to those who provide the services that support the harvesting, manufacturing, and marketing processes.

As previously stated, this arrangement leaves out a large portion of Earth's population because many people don't own land or the land they do own produces insufficient resources to provide a living, and they reside in places where the economic infrastructure does not provide jobs that allow them to earn enough to purchase what they need to sustain themselves in a viable existence. Consequently, Earth and its resources should belong to everyone, and that land and those resources should be allocated in a way that enables all human beings to obtain what they need to be viable members of the species.

The point is this: the prevalent attitude of entitlement that exists on Earth today prevents this kind of land allocation from taking place because those who presently control the land are not willing to relinquish their control, and no governmental entity presently in power is willing to ignore the influence these land owners have due to the wealth they've amassed from their holdings. Consequently, it's time to change the way land is owned and the way its resources are distributed, because until all the resources that Earth has to offer are shared so that everyone benefits equitably, there is no way to guarantee that all human beings will have the wherewithal to support themselves adequately.

Bottom line—all individuals are entitled to the means for sustaining themselves in a healthy and fruitful lifestyle, but no one has the right to prevent others from being able to do likewise by taking more than one needs.

RESOURCE DEPLETION

All human beings need to be more aware of how their chosen lifestyle affects creation's ability to continue supporting life on Earth, and they must be persuaded to willingly change those aspects of their lifestyle that impair Earth's ability to maintain the living environment upon which their well-being depends. Hopefully, when they realize that every moment of their life, every action they take depletes some of Earth's natural resources and those natural resources may or may not be replaceable, they will become more sensitive to how their behavior affects everyone's well-being. Consider breathing for example. Each time human beings take a breath, they use up a little of the oxygen in Earth's atmosphere. That means you, me, and Earth's other seven billion people use up a breath of oxygen every couple of seconds and replace it with carbon dioxide and water vapor. Now consider that all Earth's other oxygen-breathing creatures are doing the same thing. How long do you think it would take all Earth's oxygen breathers to use up all the oxygen in its atmosphere if there wasn't a way to manufacture more?

Fortunately, Earth's green plants as well as bacteria and certain oceanic organisms create oxygen constantly as a byproduct of a process called photosynthesis, which these organisms use to create the food they need to sustain themselves. Today, there are more than enough oxygen-producing organisms on Earth to satisfy the oxygen requirements of all the oxygen-breathing organisms that exist on Earth. But Earth's net human population is growing by at least 138 people per minute. That's a growth rate of over two people per second, and the growth rate for the populations of most of Earth's other oxygen-breathing organisms is the same if not greater. That means eventually the demand on Earth's oxygen will exceed Earth's oxygen-producing capacity if the oxygen-producing capacity remains unchanged.

The bad news is Earth's oxygen-producing capacity is being constantly diminished as land is cleared of its oxygen-producing plants to create the infrastructure needed to support all the activities associated with Earth's burgeoning human population. More bad news, oxygen is consumed every time combustion of natural resources is used to accomplish heating, waste disposal, and automation, and this form of oxygen consumption is also increasing at exponential rates. As a result, the balance between oxygen production and oxygen consumption is being threatened as never before. Coincidently, so is Earth's ability to maintain a temperate climate while absorbing the increasing volumes of carbon dioxide, nitrous oxide, and water vapor that are being produced during the processes of combustion and breathing. Bottom line: if people don't learn to improve their symbiotic relationship with their living environment, the quality of life on Earth will continue to deteriorate, and at some point, Earth's ability to support human life will become damaged beyond repair.

In addition, the Earth has a finite amount of natural resources, but human beings are acting as if the Earth's supply of natural resources is infinite. Most people put little thought into the amount of natural resources they consume in the course of living their lives. As previously stated, natural resources are consumed every time a human being breathes or drinks water or eats a meal. They are also consumed when any kind of implement is made or clothing is created or shelter is constructed. Therefore, it is essential that whatever is made from natural resources be created and maintained in a way that enables that product to remain functional until further use is impractical. Then, when further use becomes impractical, residual resources must be reclaimed and put to some other use.

Consider how humans typically dispose of biodegradable garbage. Most of it is dumped into landfills where it decomposes in a limited oxygen environment.

The result is ground water pollution from runoff and the production of methane gas from organic material decomposition. Methane gas is reusable as a source of energy. It has the same energy-producing component as the natural gas obtained from underground wells. The problem is, if methane gas is allowed to escape from landfills and permeate the atmosphere, it acts as a greenhouse gas and contributes to global warming. To alleviate this problem, biodegradable garbage should be disposed of in a way that prevents production of methane gas and salvages any beneficial byproducts that decomposition produces without polluting ground water. In other words, it should be disposed of in a way that prevents ground water pollution and enables the reclamation of all reusable materials including methane gas.

Since there are limited amounts of natural resources, it behooves each of us to be more conscientious in our dedication to using durable products for as long as they are serviceable then disposing of them in a way that allows reclamation of anything that can be recycled and made into something else. For example, when clothing is no longer useable, the owner should turn it in so it can be made into cleaning rags or it can be shredded and used as filler for padding or as insulation. The same is true for other types of durable products. They should not be discarded if they break or because the product is not reusable after it has served its initial purpose. If a product breaks, the owner should have it repaired and continue using it until it wears out, then it should be turned in so the materials used to construct it can be recycled and put to another use. If the product is durable but not reusable after its initial use, it should be turned in so it can be recycled and made into something else.

In other words, none of us are proactive enough in adopting a lifestyle that prolongs Earth's ability to support us. Each of us can do more to prolong the useful life of every durable product we acquire that requires consumption of additional nonrenewable natural resources if we have to replace it. By adhering to this kind of conscientious lifestyle, we not only conserve the natural resources used to manufacture the durable products we use, but also help reduce consumption of natural resources used in the mining, harvesting, processing, and manufacturing processes as well as the fuel used by the various types of mechanization that enable these processes.

Humans have to be encouraged to not let their ego, self-interest, and attitude of entitlement be the only motivational factors that influence their decision-making processes. Every time they are faced with choosing a course of action that accomplishes a desired or necessary result, they must learn to make sure that their behavior is always constructive and supportive of not only their own well-being, but also the well-being of everyone and everything else on Earth.

HEALTH MAINTENANCE

Ego also plays a role in humanity's efforts to deal with those aspects of its living environment that cause disease or some other physiological problem. Certain funguses and bacteria as well as numerous viruses threaten humanity's health because some aspect of these organisms' life cycles causes disease in the human body, and since these organisms reproduce faster than humans do, they are also able to adapt faster than humans do. As a result, even though humans have discovered ways to defend themselves against the effect these pathogens have on their physiology, they've eliminated few, if any, from continuing to be a threat. And yet, most humans ignore this threat and refuse to do the simple things that will prevent the illnesses caused by this threat. Therefore, unless they learn how to speed up their own adaptation process, humans will continue to be at risk of being overcome by one or more of these microorganisms.

CONSUMERISM

Consumers have developed a mind-set that they must have certain things to achieve their desired lifestyle. If a person has the means, it is typical for that person to replace the items they use for clothing, conveyance, and entertainment long before the end of those items' useful lives. Some people buy a whole new wardrobe each time fashions change and a new automobile whenever a new model comes out. The same is true for items used in food preparation and consumption as well as for all the other accoutrements of modern living. But what happens to the items being replaced?

Automobiles are usually traded in when they are replaced, but what about clothing and all the lesser appliances and implements commonly acquired to make life easier and more enjoyable? They shouldn't be thrown away. They should be donated to Goodwill Industries, The Salvation Army, or any other charitable organization that distributes these kinds of articles to people who are down on their luck. If you want at least some return on your investment, have a garage sale or find a recycler who'll take whatever it is that you wish to discard. Freecycle.com and craigslist.org are also great for unloading unwanted items.

The point is people love to shop, and they buy things they don't need. Then they discard stuff they already have before its useful life is over just because they prefer the latest version of whatever they're discarding. No one should discard anything durable before its useful life is over. It simply takes up space in the landfill, and since it won't decompose into anything reusable, it decreases the amount of space available for the kinds of biodegradable waste that does produce recoverable resources. The bottom line is this: as municipalities' garbage collection and landfill costs go up, they recover those costs by increasing your taxes and your fees. In other words, managing what you discard and how it is discarded not only helps conserve natural resources and prevent environmental pollution, it keeps money in your pocket.

Changing your mind-set regarding durable product use and disposal can also be rewarding to you monetarily, and it can be rewarding from a humanitarian point of view as well. Creation is forever. On the other hand, individual human beings and the human species have a finite life expectancy. However, the length and quality of that lifetime depend on the choices each member of the species makes. If humans learn to control those actions that lead to a disruption in the natural balance of their own physiology, and they learn to curtail those actions that disrupt the natural balance in creation, individual lives will be longer, healthier, and more enjoyable. However, this objective can only be accomplished if all human beings learn to place less importance on their personal agendas and more importance on behavior that results in enhancing Earth's ability to support all human life at a desirable level for an indefinite period of time.

CHAPTER 4

Societal Issues Caused By Misguided Child-nurturing Practices

One of the most critical areas that needs to be addressed to bring about a universally cohesive human society is the way parents raise their children. There is presently no consistency in what is considered acceptable child-rearing practices. In fact, there are an almost infinite number of opinions on this subject, and all are self-perpetuating because parents fail to understand two basic principles. The first is that children emulate the behavior of their mentors, and the most influential mentors during a child's formative years are the child's parents as well as the other adults with whom the child has a close relationship—for example, grandparents, aunts, uncles, etc. Regardless of who raises them, children tend to raise their children using the same techniques that were used on them, and thus, bad child-raising procedures get perpetuated.

The second is that it's human nature for infants to rebel against any attempt to control their behavior that prevents them from doing what they want to do. In fact, such efforts usually reinforce infants' determination to have their way. That's because human beings are naturally inclined to rebel against any effort to control their behavior, and they never lose that inclination. Fortunately, as most of us grow into maturity, we learn how to acquiesce to behavior-controlling efforts to whatever extent is necessary to avoid treatment that is beyond our tolerance for pain and inconvenience. In other words, most of us learn to moderate our behavior to the extent necessary to peacefully coexist, first with the people who are responsible for raising us and later with all the people we must deal with as we go about living our lives. Nevertheless, to a greater or lesser extent, none of us learn to completely suppress our rebellious nature.

Therefore, the problem that continues to challenge humanity is finding a way to obtain desirable human behavior without having to resort to fear tactics. In the 1960s in the United States and elsewhere, the hippie movement was somewhat successful in advocating "love" as the answer. But the primary intent when promoting "love" as being all you need was primarily to promote a form of rebellion intended to enable people to have greater freedom to pursue behavioral interests that prevailing societal mores forbade. In other words, the hippies were advocating freedom to enjoy carnal pleasures, primarily. Their secondary objective was making changes essential to attaining world peace.

Nevertheless, the movement was important in that it demonstrated yet again that people who choose to pursue a different lifestyle than that which is more universally accepted can do so by using peaceful disobedience techniques rather than by resorting to physical violence. A similar tactic is presently being used by protesters in Egypt and elsewhere where they are attempting to force changes in the way they are being governed. Their objective is to eliminate the special interest politics that have enriched the few at the expense of the majority.

The point is, once a person or a group of people decide that no force or influence will keep them from advocating for a freedom that they believe is reasonable, the use of force becomes futile and will eventually be abandoned, particularly if public opinion supports the position being advocated. Of course, maintaining law and order is essential to enabling a society of human beings to peacefully coexist with one another. Therefore, the objective is to establish a society in which people are free to pursue their interests as long as what they choose to do isn't harmful to themselves or to others or to some aspect of Earth's environment that is essential in providing a safe and healthy living environment.

Obviously, the establishment of such a society must begin with everyone having a better understanding of which kinds of behavior are harmful and which are not. The first step is to establish the mind-set that any kind of behavior that causes premature death or permanent debilitation is unacceptable, even if the cause is accidental. In other words, people must be made to understand that intentionally engaging in behavior that is directly or indirectly responsible for rendering someone incapable of normal functionality is a violation subject to escalating penalties for repeat offenders. This behavioral restriction includes behavior that, if engaged in over some period of time, has a debilitating effect on the perpetrator or on bystanders who are affected by the side effects of such behavior.

Similarly, the establishment of such a society must include the expectation that all persons who are responsible for raising an infant will adhere to a common method of teaching the children in their care what is and is not acceptable behavior. Until humanity adopts a universally accepted way of teaching children how to interact with those they meet, prejudice, differences in religious beliefs, and differences in social status will be stumbling blocks to ensuring that human beings discontinue repeating the mistakes of the past over and over again.

If we want world peace, everyone has to eliminate the "my way or the highway" attitude prevalent today. All people should be allowed to choose the lifestyle they wish to follow as long as it allows them to live peacefully and harmlessly with everyone and everything else on Earth. Such an attitude is essential if humanity is ever going to evolve into a worldwide community of individuals who tolerate each others' ways of doing things as long as the path chosen doesn't impede Earth or any of its occupants from being the best they can be.

CHAPTER 5
Eliminating Societal Issues Caused by Expedient Behavior

The thing that has enabled human beings to successfully inhabit and thrive almost everywhere on Earth is their ability to increase their knowledge and understanding of how things work while trying new ways to solve whatever problems impede them from accomplishing the desired objective, whether it is being able to live in extreme weather conditions comfortably or getting from starting point to objective as quickly, efficiently, and effectively as possible. In other words, human beings have always sought ways to make life easier and more enjoyable.

Recently some have begun to realize that the inventions they've embraced that make life easier and more enjoyable actually represent a threat to the well-being of some, if not all, human beings. Therefore, the anticipated benefits of a new invention must not cause the inventor or the users of that invention to ignore the possibility that the product's production or use may produce residues or cause damage that adversely affects some aspect of creation on Earth. Fortunately, at least some inventors and consumers are beginning to be more deliberate in considering the effect on Earth's environment and its organisms that contemplated products may have, and they are beginning to eliminate those products and procedures that are known to have undesirable side effects.

Obviously, the Earth will not be a completely healthy place to live until everyone commits to eliminate all behavior and procedures that adversely affect Earth's ability to continue supporting human life. Therefore, laws must be implemented worldwide that influence people to make the kinds of decisions in achieving their desired lifestyle that assure the preferable outcome, namely, that the human species will learn how to behave in a way that ensures the health and well-being of its species for an indefinite period of time.

SECTION 2

Aspects of Human Nature That Make Peace on Earth Attainable

Human beings who are aware, inquisitive, inventive, intelligent, and empathetic are better able to communicate with one another. These attributes when coupled with humanity's innate self-interest offer hope that all is not lost. Human awareness helps them recognize when things are not working as they should be. Their inquisitiveness helps them understand what needs to be done to make things work better. Their intelligence and inventiveness help them create solutions to perceived problems. Their ability to communicate enables them to rectify previous misunderstandings and stimulate enlightened thought. And their empathy enables them to care about the well-being of others. All that's left is for all humans to realize that their own health and well-being, as well as the survival of their species, depends on every aspect of planet Earth functioning in ways that enhance rather than diminish Earth's ability to support human life. This is particularly true with regard to improving humanity's ability to peacefully coexist with one another, because every human being has the potential to contribute genetically, mentally, and physically toward improving the species' ability to exist on Earth effectively.

CHAPTER 6

Every Human Being Contributes to Humanity's Legacy

All human beings play a role in helping their species survive because at the moment each human being is conceived, the genetic material provided by the mother and the father is combined in a way that creates a new human being whose genetic makeup is unique and may contribute in some way to developing a bodily capability that was not previously present in any other human being who had ever existed. Identical twins are the exception, but even they respond differently to the various types of stimuli they experience during their lifetimes. In other words, the genetic material responsible for creating each person's physical and mental characteristics is unique. Consequently, it's probable that every individual's physical or mental characteristics will include the genetic coding for some capability that was not present in either parent or in any other human previously conceived. Furthermore, that capability may enable people who have it to handle some aspect of their living environment better than anyone else had been able to do previously, and when that's the case, individuals who possess this capability will be more successful at surviving in their living environment and therefore more likely to successfully propagate thereby passing their unique body characteristics on to the next generation.

Ultimately, if generation after generation inherits such a capability, the genes that create this beneficial body characteristic will permeate the entire group of individuals who are exposed to the particular environmental living conditions that exist in the place where they live. For example, some human beings have dark skin because their ancestors originated in areas where they were constantly exposed to intense sunlight. Over time, a different kind of melanin evolved in their skin's epidermis and that variety of melanin makes the skin dark. This variety of melanin is commonly found in people indigenous to the landmasses located along the equator and twenty degrees either side of it where the sun's ultraviolet radiation is the most intense.

Usually, the benefit derived from a new bodily characteristic may not be apparent in the person whose genes create it, and it may not manifest itself unless that person has offspring and the offspring have offspring, etc. Unfortunately, it is not possible presently to detect at birth how new human beings will turn out or whether they possess a physical characteristic that may ultimately enhance humanity's ability to continue its existence on Earth and to better enjoy the time during which we exist on Earth. To ensure that all human beings who are born into this world are given every opportunity to flourish and to contribute whatever gifts they may possess or may accomplish to humanity, all people must be properly nurtured and must be allowed to live out their lives to their natural conclusions.

Furthermore, humans must develop and implement procedures that enable them to identify, save, and replicate genetic coding that is known to develop a unique body characteristic enabling human beings who have it to function more effectively in their living environments. They must also change their social attitudes regarding the value of an individual's life by teaching everyone that intentionally causing the death of any human being from the point of conception to the point of natural demise is completely unacceptable. Otherwise, who knows how much of humanity's ultimate potential will be irrevocably lost before it has a chance to manifest itself.

Another lesson that must be taught to everyone universally is that people who have bodily characteristics noticeably different from their own should not be considered to be freaks of nature. Instead, they should be considered to be possible precursors for an improvement in body functionality that may eventually improve all humans' ability to deal with a harmful aspect of their living environment. In other words, everyone should be considered to be the potential originator of a bodily characteristic improvement that, if passed on to progeny, will eventually benefit all human beings indigenous to an area where people who do not have this bodily characteristic are adversely affected in a way that impairs their functionality, sometimes to the point of causing them to die.

Conclusion: it behooves all human beings to commit to doing whatever they can to ensure that other human beings receive proper nurturing and are protected from all behavior that diminishes their physical or mental functionality and causes them to die prematurely. If we don't, we risk the possibility that whatever contribution to humanity people's unique physical and mental capabilities allow them to make will be lost. That's because the manifestation of one individual's unique genetic attributes may never occur in anyone else, and if that turns out to be the case, humanity will be deprived of the enrichment those attributes and abilities might have contributed.

CHAPTER 7

Proper Nurturing Ensures Every Human's Contribution to Humanity

As mentioned in chapter 6, all human beings have the potential when they are born to develop into individuals who contribute in some way to improving the human species or to improving the quality of life that humans experience during their lifetimes. By properly nurturing every human being from birth to maturity and giving individuals every opportunity to contribute whatever gifts they have that may ultimately help improve the quality of life all humans experience during their lifetime on Earth, humanity can achieve universal well-being.

Proper nurturing involves ensuring that people are properly nourished and that their minds and bodies are exercised sufficiently to sustain healthy functionality. Other aspects of nurturing include ensuring that all people thoroughly understand what is and is not acceptable behavior in interactions with others and with their living environment and ensuring that they are able to reconcile their interests and capabilities to select a life's work that enables them to contribute positively to humanity's successful existence. The proper nurturing of an individual is not only the responsibility of an individual's parents and immediate family, but also of every other person who is influential in the development of that individual into a fully functioning person. If you've raised a child, you know that a baby's total focus is on its own needs and comfort. That self-absorption is essential to its survival. But as soon as a baby is able to understand, he or she must be taught to switch from being self-absorbed to being aware that his or her needs are no more important than the needs of other members of his or her immediate family. Eventually, the child must also learn that his or her needs are no more important than those of everyone and everything else with whom he or she shares life on Earth.

Human beings want to do the things that make them feel good, and they avoid doing things that have the opposite effect. Unfortunately, there are bad things that cause good feelings and good things that cause bad feelings. For example, few people enjoy eating the variety of fruits and vegetables needed to maintain their health and physical functionality. For optimum nutritional value it is preferable to eliminate as much processing, seasoning, and cooking as possible, but most people prefer eating foods that have been overcooked and heavily seasoned with added sugar, salt, and fat, even though scientists have proved that heavy doses of sugar, salt, and fat in the diet create health problems and that overcooking reduces food's nutritional value.

Since most people's eating habits and other behaviors are established during their childhood, it is incumbent on all parents and on society as a whole to be consistent in teaching all children to do the things that produce the best results regarding their health and well-being as well as their ability to function effectively within the society in which they live. This is best accomplished if all people who interact with children set a good example by making sure all behavior that they engage in while in a child's presence is consistent with the kind of behavior all children are expected to emulate. Without this consistency, a child is likely to witness behavioral contradictions that will be confusing, particularly if such behavior fails to elicit disapproval from the adults present when such contradictions take place. In most families, children are exposed via books, radio programs, movies, and television to strangers acting out behavior that contradicts the kinds of behavior in which the child is expected to engage. Therefore, parents who allow such exposure are sending mixed signals to their children, and unless that changes, no amount of discipline by parents will prevent their children from choosing a lifestyle that is incompatible with what's best for the overall well-being of society as a whole.

It is essential that all children are taught to be considerate of others, and it is also essential that all adults be taught to make sure that all interactions with others that are observed by an impressionable young person are consistent with the way the child is expected to interact with others. Otherwise, confusion ensues and undermines the child's willingness to accept what the child is being taught as being acceptable behavior. This is particularly true when supposedly unacceptable behavior being engaged in by others in the child's presence appears to be approved of, or at least condoned, by those who are trying to teach the child how to behave acceptably. In other words, parents and all others who interact with impressionable children must try to avoid exposing those children to behavior that contradicts the lessons the children are supposed to be learning.

SECTION 3

Suggestions for Enhancing Earth's and Humanity's Well-being

The following chapters suggest changes in the way humans do things that enhance their well-being either directly or indirectly. The objective is to introduce new ideas for actions that can improve humanity's ability to adapt to the ever-changing environmental conditions that exist on Earth and eliminate actions and behavioral attitudes that degrade environmental conditions rather than enhancing them.

CHAPTER 8

Constructive Societal Behavior Must Be Adhered to by Everyone

Societal behavior begins with the way a society's children are taught what is and is not acceptable. Children are inquisitive creatures who are constantly aware of how others are reacting to their own appearance, behavior, manner of speaking, and types of words used. Babies are constantly observing the way parents and siblings behave amongst themselves and with others while in their presence. In adolescence, children broaden their awareness of the ways people act toward and react to other people by observing how others behave. The behavior they witness may be firsthand or it may be via movies, books, magazines, television, and radio. For example, behavior and styles of clothing worn by anyone perceived to be a role model tends to be emulated by impressionable young individuals who are seeking to establish their own personal identity and to gain the attention of those whose attention they covet.

Children's parents, siblings, teachers, and others who regularly interact with them can reinforce acceptable behavior by using each child's need for attention to reinforce that child's perception of what they should and shouldn't do. In other words, everyone with whom a child interacts on a regular basis must either show that child love or withhold it to obtain the desired result. Of course, this tactic is most effective when all persons who are important to a child project the same expectations and react in a consistent manner. This consistency helps the child develop the kind of character the child will need in order to become a fully accepted member of the child's extended family as well as society as a whole.

Parents and other influential persons in a child's life must also use their behavior to demonstrate how the child should interact with people who are not part of the child's immediate or extended family. In other words, every person with whom a child interacts should be consistently practicing the "Golden Rule" by treating others the same way the person wishes to be treated. If everyone in the world decided to follow this simple formula, Earth would be filled with people who have learned how to peacefully coexist with one another. As a result, no one would feel threatened by anyone's opinion regarding religion, politics, choice of attire, lifestyle, etc. Instead, all people would accept that everyone else has the same rights they do, namely to live life as the person chooses, provided the person does nothing that harms oneself, others, or Earth's ability to function properly.

CHAPTER 9

Destructive Societal Behavior Must Be Eliminated

All of us need to think seriously about how what we do in the course of living our lives impacts Earth's ability to support human life. To start, I'd like to offer some observations as food for thought beginning with the obvious. Every time we take in a breath of air, we use up a little of the oxygen in the Earth's atmosphere. As mentioned previously, that means every one of Earth's seven billion people as well as all other oxygen-breathing organisms is taking oxygen out of the air every couple of seconds and replacing it with carbon dioxide and water vapor.

So why don't we run out of oxygen, and why doesn't the carbon dioxide and water vapor exhaled by all those oxygen-breathing creatures accumulate in the atmosphere and contribute to global warming? As you probably already know, it's because Earth's green plants as well as certain kinds of bacteria and oceanic organisms are constantly creating oxygen as a byproduct of the complicated chemical process called photosynthesis, which these organisms use to produce the food they require to sustain themselves. It gets better. Guess what one of the raw materials is that photosynthesis requires? Carbon dioxide! In other words, organisms that use photosynthesis to manufacture their food take carbon dioxide out of the air and water from the ground and put both oxygen and water vapor back into the atmosphere. Is that symbiosis or what? Therefore, as long as there are sufficient organisms existing on Earth that use the carbon dioxide that air-breathing organisms produce to produce the oxygen that air-breathing organisms require, all is well.

However, we humans are inventive sorts, and we've created lots of ways to make life more enjoyable. In fact, almost every human endeavor these days involves activities that result in oxygen being taken out of the atmosphere and replaced with carbon dioxide and other greenhouse gases. Plus, as living has become easier, the human population has exploded. Consequently, more land is being cleared to accommodate the needs of all these people. Guess what populations are being diminished by this change in land use? The answer is carbon dioxide-removing, oxygen-producing green plants. Furthermore, the residue from all these pollution-producing activities is reducing the effectiveness of Earth's lakes and oceans as a living environment for organisms that use photosynthesis to produce oxygen. It is also adversely affecting water-bound organisms that use carbon dioxide absorbed from the atmosphere to build the shells they use to protect themselves from predators. In the latter case, that's really serious because the carbon dioxide sequestered in these organisms' shells is taken out of the loop indefinitely.

Why are these facts important? Have you heard about the greenhouse effect? You are probably familiar with the all-glass buildings called greenhouses that people use to grow plants that require climate-controlled conditions. These buildings let sunlight create the warm environment plants need to be healthy organisms, and they are vented to keep it from getting too hot inside. Well, Earth's atmosphere functions much like the glass in a greenhouse in the sense that it lets the sunlight through to warm the air near the Earth's surface and keeps that warmth from escaping back into space.

Unlike a glass greenhouse, though, Earth's greenhouse effect is not easily regulated because the accumulation of greenhouse gases in Earth's atmosphere is not easily controlled. So if activities on Earth continue to put more and more carbon dioxide and other greenhouse gasses into the atmosphere, less heat is able to escape. As a result, temperatures at the Earth's surface begin to rise beyond the temperate range within which Earth's ecosystems operate efficiently. That's not good.

Temperate climate, breathable air, and unpolluted water are not the only aspects of Earth's ability to support human life that are in jeopardy. The Earth has finite amounts of the kinds of natural resources that are used to create the raw materials humans use to produce the things they need to sustain their existence. In order to make those resources last as long as possible, all people must learn as early as possible to regard all natural resources and all things made from natural resources as being precious, and they must be taught to limit their consumption of natural resources to what is necessary to support themselves in a universally accepted standard of living. In addition, they must be taught how to extend the useful life of all the durable products they use that are made from natural resources.

Societal expectations should be that all people will limit their consumption of natural resources and the products made from natural resources to the amount of clothing and other accoutrements needed to sustain an acceptable lifestyle given the economic and climatic circumstances for the geographic area or areas in which an individual resides and works. Acquisition of additional clothing and any other accoutrements of an acceptable lifestyle should not be necessary unless a durable product they already own can no longer serve its purpose and is no longer repairable. In addition to clothing, the accoutrements needed to sustain an acceptable lifestyle include such items as a nonpolluting, energy-efficient dwelling and adequate modes of transportation as well as the various implements used to maintain mental health, physical health, and optimal productivity in all endeavors.

Society's expectation should also be that people adopt healthy eating habits and consume only nutritious food in amounts sufficient to maintain their bodies in their optimum functional condition. All people will also be expected to exercise their bodies to the extent needed to maintain muscle and bone functionality as well as physique stability. This will enable them to minimize the need to replace clothing because their physiques have changed. Of course, a person's body grows and shrinks with age and activity, and there are maladies that affect a person's physique, so an exchange program must be implemented so individuals can deal with these kinds of changes without having to acquire new garments when such changes occur unless there is a shortage of comparable garments in the size needed.

Similarly, everyone should be expected to make do with one of all the other durable goods required to support an acceptable lifestyle. In addition to the items previously listed, this means owning one set of cooking utensils, one television set, and all the other durable products used to accomplish an acceptable standard of living. Such diligence in acquiring these kinds of durable products and properly maintaining them in order to prolong their useful lives will significantly reduce the consumption of nonrenewable natural resources. And it will prolong Earth's ability to supply the nonrenewable natural resources required to replace durable products when they reach the point at which further maintenance will no longer restore their effectiveness.

Reducing the need to produce new products also reduces consumption of fuel used during the harvesting, transporting, and converting of natural resources into components and end products, and it reduces the consumption of fuel used to distribute these manufactured items to their various destinations. Reductions in fuel consumption also reduce the volume of hazardous residues being produced by fuel combustion as well as the expenditure of nonrenewable resources used to capture and eliminate these residues and counteract the effect these residues have on the health and well-being of human beings and Earth's ecology. Furthermore, when products are made from plastics, synthetic cloth, or other materials derived from oil and gas, not only are the aforementioned reductions realized when fewer new products are produced, the hazardous residues from the processes used to manufacture these synthetic materials will also be reduced. In summary, adjusting attitudes regarding the acquisition, use, and disposition of durable goods made from natural resources will prolong Earth's ability to support human life and will dramatically enhance and improve the length and quality of humanity's time on Earth.

So, what can each of us do to help solve these problems? If you read a newspaper, listen to talk radio, or watch the news and infomercials on TV, you're being constantly bombarded with expert opinions, but the bottom line is simple.

Until each of us becomes constantly aware of how every action we take affects Earth's ability to function effectively, and until each of us commits to eliminate all behavior and activities that adversely affect Earth's ability to function effectively, the continued survival of our species is not assured.

CHAPTER 10
Natural Selection Must Be Helped To Enhance Human Functionality

Humans need to speed up their ability to counteract external influences that have a detrimental effect on their health and well-being. To do that they must learn how to manipulate the adaptation process that enables their bodies to resist the effects of external influences that adversely affect their physiology. By managing their reproduction, they can reproduce chance variations in the genetic material that enables people who have it to resist a known pathogen or become more physiologically adept. Once an effective genetic variation has been identified, it can be introduced into all succeeding offspring of all members of the species so they will be impervious to the effects of that influence. This will enhance the chances that everyone born afterward will be more disease resistant and more physiologically sound than might otherwise be the case.

Since each species perpetuates itself through reproduction, and reproduction involves chemical interactions that are controlled by genetic coding, errors in the copying process involved in creating a new individual can result in an individual whose genetic coding produces a beneficial bodily characteristic. Occasionally, this new bodily characteristic enables the person who has it to become better adapted to an aspect of the person's living environment that otherwise would threaten the person's viability.

This process is known as genetic mutation, and once a beneficial genetic mutation occurs, it is very likely that the individual who has it will pass it on to its progeny, but it only gets passed to that individual's next generation, not every new individual of the species. Consequently it takes a very long time for a new bodily characteristic to manifest itself throughout a species or subspecies. That's because the new characteristic must bestow some advantage on those who have it that makes their ability to reproduce more likely than those that don't have it. Consequently, people with beneficial or appealing bodily characteristics will be the ones who are more likely to pass on their genetic coding to the next generation. Eventually, this process will enable a beneficial bodily characteristic to permeate an entire species or create a new sub species. But the process takes hundreds of thousands of generations of successfully passing on the mutated genetic coding for a beneficial bodily characteristic before it permeates an entire species or creates a new sub species.

Humans need to learn how to speed this process up by using modern scientific and medical procedures. If humans began to keep physiological records on all individuals from their birth to their death, an analysis could be made of their response to health-threatening events that occurred during their lifetime in the places on Earth where they lived. This kind of data would enable researchers to identify individuals who are born with a genetic variation that enables them to be more physiologically successful than contemporaries who live in similar environmental circumstances. Once one or more individual survivors have been identified, their DNA can be analyzed to determine if the same genetic anomaly may have contributed to their survivability. Then, when enough evidence has been collected to confirm the anomaly's contribution in improving viability, it can then be replicated and made part of the genetic makeup of all who are born afterward if their genetic makeup does not already include the coding for that genetic anomaly. This procedure will speed up humanity's ability to respond to changes in its living environment that threaten its existence. Plus, when coupled with the continued development of medicines, humanity's ability to maintain its viability on Earth and beyond it will be significantly improved.

Some may argue that the proposed procedure will tend to make all humans identical and that contradicts the evolutionary process. To the contrary, the proposed system depends on the random comingling of genetic material from the two mating individuals and on the randomness of the way in which the genetic material contributed by both participants is combined. The difference is that, if the genetic material of the resulting embryo does not contain all the genetic coding known to make the resulting human being impervious to the effects of known pathogens, environmental influences, and physiological problems, those variations can be introduced so that the resulting children will be more likely to reach maturity and pass their own genetic variations to the next generation.

In order to initiate the proposed procedure, it would be necessary to establish a worldwide repository of DNA samples obtained from every existing human being so that, if it is determined after death that the individual who died has a genetic variation that improves human responsiveness to pathogenic threats or enhances human performance in stressful environmental circumstances, that genetic variation can be introduced into all embryos created after those determinations have been made. The beauty of this approach is that even people who don't produce their own children will still be able to contribute whatever is different in their DNA that might enhance humanity's ability to continue adapting to Earth's ever-changing environmental conditions.

Obviously, enhancing natural selection requires that every human being who is conceived is allowed to develop into a fully functioning, reproductive adult. This is best accomplished by ensuring that all individuals who are born are properly nurtured and allowed to grow up in an environment in which their safety and health are assured. Otherwise, the possibility that the unique genetic coding that enables one person's body to function more effectively may be lost before any genetic improvements can be identified and used to improve the survivability of the entire human species.

CHAPTER 11

All Humans Are Homo sapiens (i.e., Members of the Same Family)

The following are various considerations regarding what must be done to reconcile the fact that all human beings are essential to humanity's ability to remain viable on Earth with the fact that most humans today are only concerned with acquiring the goods and services needed to sustain themselves in the most desirable lifestyle possible given their economic status. It is presently impossible to ensure that every individual human who is born on Earth will be able to live a full, productive life. That means some human beings will never get the opportunity to make whatever contribution to improving the quality and duration of humanity's existence on Earth that their unique capabilities might have enabled them to make. That's because the circumstances of their existence are such that they are not able to obtain the wherewithal to sustain a healthy, productive lifestyle.

It is essential that all people understand that it's in their best interests to make sure everyone, including themselves, is allowed to live out their life to its natural conclusion and be given every opportunity during that lifetime to play their role in improving the viability of the human species and the quality of human existence on Earth. This can be accomplished if all people resolve to make sure that the way they do things and the way things are done by others is consistent with the way things must be done to achieve the desired outcome, namely, sustaining the health and well-being of the entire human species.

Asking people to do things the way they should be done because that's what's best for the species may be too abstract to motivate some people to change the way they presently do things. Most people only change behavioral habits when they understand why doing so benefits them directly. Therefore the argument for why they should do things a certain way has to relate to an aspect of their lives that is important to them. For example, almost everyone instinctively cares about his or her own familial legacy. In other words, almost all people want to produce children and then have their children produce grandchildren. If they don't have children of their own, they have siblings who have children and whose children have children, so almost everyone has a personal interest in the well-being of the small group of human beings with whom they are genetically related. In such instances, people are usually willing to do whatever they can to ensure that those particular human beings get along in the world as well as possible. This aspect of human nature is instinctive. Because of its instinctive nature, this common interest can be used to motivate a large segment of Earth's population to be more mindful of how their behavior affects not only themselves, but also all the other people in the world who are important to them.

In other words, when people realize they have something in common with every other human being in the world, namely, the safety and well-being of their own family, they'll be more likely to be willing to engage only in behavior that doesn't adversely affect anyone or anything else with whom they share this planet. That's because all people will understand that their genetic relatives are simply a subset of the human race and that all the familial subsets of human beings on Earth are essential in enabling future generations to remain viable on Earth. And when that realization comes to fruition, people will begin to regard even strangers as members of their extended family and they will begin to treat them with the same civility and give them the same consideration as that which they give to members of their own, more immediate, genetically related family.

SECTION 4
Earth and Its Natural Resources Must Be Preserved

As far as we know, there is not another planet in our universe that can do what Earth is able to do, namely, support oxygen-breathing, carbon-based organisms that require potable water for survival. Since human beings are such organisms, we need to accept that there aren't any viable alternatives to making life on Earth work. Therefore, all human beings must be made to understand, as early in their lives as possible, that Earth's natural resources and all things made from natural resources are precious and must be preserved because the supply of nonrenewable natural resources that humans rely on for survival is limited to what exists on and within planet Earth. When they're used up, we're done. But humanity may never have to worry about that eventuality, because Earth's capacity for absorbing the pollution humans are creating may be exhausted first, and we'll have already expired from suffocation. That's because Earth's air will have become no longer breathable or because the increasing heat at the Earth's surface caused by the greenhouse effect will have become intolerable.

Due to ignorance or eternal optimism, most people dismiss these doomsday scenarios as scare tactics, because neither of these scenarios is likely to happen today, tomorrow, next year or even during their lifetimes, and that's all most of us are concerned about. On the other hand, our natural inclination is to propagate our genes to ensure our species' immortality, so shouldn't each of us be concerned about protecting the well-being of our own future generations? Unless we ensure, as much as possible, that Earth's living environment will support them, why should we bring more children into this world and force them to face the unpleasant task of making do with limited resources while trying to survive in an ever hotter, more toxic living environment?

What are the alternatives? Should we keep doing what we're doing and hope for the best? Or should we begin a concerted effort to convince all humans alive today that limiting their consumption of natural resources will ensure that some is left for future generations? Why not limit ourselves to consuming only that which is adequate to sustain a universally accepted standard of living and do everything we can to extend the useful life of all the durable products made from natural resources we use to make life easier? Diminishing the need for new products reduces the depletion of natural resources. Furthermore, since Earth's ability to absorb pollution is finite, why aren't humans doing everything they can to reduce the amount of environmental pollution they create as a byproduct of their efforts to maintain a satisfactory lifestyle? Every living organism requires unpolluted air, soil, and water to sustain its health and functionality.

The bottom line: unless we address these concerns soon, life on Earth will become more and more problematic.

CHAPTER 12

Durable Products Must Never Be Discarded

As stated previously, no durable product should be discarded as trash. Furthermore, manufacturers of durable products such as appliances, vehicles, dwellings, and implements should create the most long-lasting products possible rather than create products that stop working after a short time, thereby forcing the consumer to spend money on repairs or buy replacements more often. Manufacturers should also avoid marketing practices that tempt consumers to trade in serviceable products for replacements that perform the same function but have a more appealing appearance. Consumers, on the other hand, should learn how to use the things they buy in the most fuel-efficient, cost-effective way possible and to maintain those things so they last as long as possible.

Of course, manufacturers must constantly endeavor to improve the efficiency, effectiveness, and durability of the products they make. But this presents consumers with a dilemma, which is whether to keep using a product they already own that is less efficient, effective, and durable or trade it in when an improved version becomes available. This dilemma can be solved by implementing a program that requires manufacturers to make only one version of a product and if a product has multiple parts, to design the product so that all parts involved in making the product more efficient and effective can be replaced with parts that produce improvements in that product's efficiency and effectiveness without having to reconstruct the whole product. This requirement will allow less efficient or effective parts of a product to be upgraded when improvements are developed, and this will reduce the consumption of natural resources that would otherwise be required to manufacture whole product replacements when improvements in efficiency and effectiveness are developed.

In summary, manufacturers and consumers alike must become more resolute in their efforts to conserve natural resources by continually upgrading existing products with replaceable parts and components that improve a product's energy efficiency, functionality, and durability. To avoid becoming bored with expensive products like houses and automobiles before their usefulness ends, owners will be permitted occasional cosmetic changes such as fresh paint and swapping out floor, furniture, and wall coverings. But under no circumstances should anyone be allowed to replace durable products until they've worn out or have been destroyed by unavoidable calamity.

In order to get everyone to pay attention to these matters, a worldwide organization must be established that enlists people who are committed to encouraging everyone to willingly limit their consumption of natural resources and the products made from them to that which is adequate to sustain a universally accepted standard of living. To become involved, people simply have to formally commit to living by example and to being proactive in encouraging others to do the same.

Imagine how much of a reduction in the depletion of Earth's natural resources and in the pollution of Earth's living environment could be achieved if all people willingly limited the clothing they own to the amount needed to sustain a universally accepted standard of living? And what if they limited the other accoutrements of their lifestyle to nonpolluting, energy-efficient products that provide a place to live, a means of transportation, and one each of the various implements needed to accomplish the various activities associated with maintaining one's household as well as one's physical well-being and productivity?

Reducing the need to produce new products will also reduce consumption of fuel used during the harvesting, transporting, and converting of natural resources into components and end products, and it will reduce the consumption of fuel used to distribute these manufactured items to their various destinations. Secondarily, reductions in fuel consumption will reduce the volume of hazardous residues being produced by fuel combustion, reduce the amount of nonrenewable resources used to capture and eliminate these residues, and reduce the effect these residues have on the health and well-being of human beings and Earth's ecology. Furthermore, reducing production of new products made from materials that are derivatives of oil and gas, like plastics and synthetic cloth for example, not only accomplishes the aforementioned reductions, it reduces the hazardous residues produced by the processes used to manufacture these synthetic materials.

To be sure, these proposed changes are radical departures from the way things are done today in the areas of the world where people can afford to be extravagant. But imagine what would happen if such requirements were imposed worldwide? Economies would become less driven by consumerism and by the marketing/advertising industry whose business it is to stimulate and encourage consumerism. All-encompassing exchange stores would replace retail outlets that specialize in specific merchandise, the infinite variety of consumer outlets that vie for the consumer's dollar would be eliminated, and manufacturers would produce new products only when existing products needed to be replaced because they could no longer be improved with parts that produce the effectiveness and efficiency of newly designed replacements.

The focus of manufacturing would be on producing products that can be upgraded without having to replace the whole product, but researchers would continue to try to discover ways to accomplish tasks using more effective and efficient means.

In other words, durable goods' sole purpose should be to enable people to accomplish life's necessary tasks in the most effective way possible while minimizing the amount of natural resources consumed and the waste produced during their creation as well as throughout their useful life. Once the infrastructure has been changed to make this happen, the next step would be to change the way Earth's natural resources are owned and distributed to ensure that all Earth's human beings are able to obtain the natural resources and products made from natural resources that are required to adequately sustain their well-being and viability.

CHAPTER 13

Earth's Natural Resources Must Be Shared Equitably

In the book *The Science of Good & Evil*, Michael Shermer claims that disparate groups, who might otherwise go to war with one another because one group has something the other group needs, will tend to peacefully coexist if they learn how to trade with one another to obtain what they need rather than take it by force. What if all human beings on Earth could learn to share Earth's natural resources and the produce of those natural resources equitably? The world would become a community in which all people are able to sustain themselves in a viable existence. What's preventing that from happening? Individual human beings who are unwilling to acknowledge that all Earth's natural resources should belong to everyone and that the products created from those resources should be distributed in a way that enables all Earth's residents to benefit equally.

Since the Earth's resources are not evenly distributed geographically, some areas have an abundance of natural resources while other areas have a paucity of natural resources. Regardless, given Earth's present geopolitical structure, there are few countries in the world in which all citizens have the wherewithal to support themselves in an adequate lifestyle. That's because of the way resources are owned and distributed in most countries. Therefore, the way natural resources are owned and distributed needs to be changed, and that means national sovereignty can no longer extend to the natural resources found within the area claimed by each nation.

Consider the issue presently being discussed in a conference of nations whose sovereignty extends to land bordering the Arctic Sea. They are arguing over which country owns the rights to the huge deposits of natural gas located there. Consider also the long-standing understanding that whoever owns a piece of land also owns the natural resource on or below that land unless they've sold those rights to someone else. In both instances, the benefits derived from those natural resources are not distributed in a way that benefits everyone equitably.

Why should luck and antiquated laws be involved in determining who benefits from natural resource extraction and who doesn't? It shouldn't. In fact, all of Earth's natural resources should be owned by all human beings and used to ensure that every human being and every life form that human survival depends on has enough of Earth's land, its natural resources, and the produce of those natural resources to sustain their viability.

In order to do that, every human being on Earth must recognize that they and all other humans constitute a worldwide community of the same species and that the survival of a species depends on every one of its members having the opportunity to thrive. Therefore, Earth's resources need to be more effectively and efficiently utilized so that all human beings, regardless of where on Earth they live, are able to achieve a healthy, productive standard of living in an environment that is as supportive of healthy living as possible. That objective is achievable when everyone learns to respect and care about others as much as they expect others to respect and care about them, because, in the final analysis, the well-being of all life on Earth depends on the symbiotic relationships that every individual organism has with all the other organisms that are essential to its survival.

CHAPTER 14

Land Must Be Allocated Equitably

Any individual who is conceived and born may possess unique genetic coding that creates an improved bodily characteristic. Therefore, it is imperative that every human be allowed to thrive and have progeny. This will improve the chances that a variation in one individual's genetic coding that improves bodily functionality may eventually improve the bodily functionality of every member of the human species. To enhance the chances of that happening, everyone must be allowed to benefit equally from the use of Earth's land and its natural resources.

Obviously, the first priority is to allocate sufficient land to grow the crops used for human sustenance and for the sustenance of the animals that humans rely upon for food, clothing, and other purposes. Land must also be allocated for all aspects of societal infrastructure that enable and support human productivity. Finally, land with attributes that make it enjoyable to view and make it a place that inspires enjoyable interactions with nature must be set aside and preserved for recreational use by everyone.

Today, the great majority of people living on Earth struggle to eke out a living that is sufficient to adequately support themselves and any family they might have. Most have insufficient land to grow what they need or they live in places where no work is available that would enable them to earn enough to adequately support themselves and their family. In other words, a significant portion of the world's human population have few options in their struggle for survival other than to scavenge, beg, steal, or prostitute themselves. This is the biggest problem to be solved if all people on Earth are to be assured of having everything they need to sustain an adequate lifestyle. Obviously, the solution involves changing the way land is owned and used, but it also involves teaching all people the skills and knowledge they need to engage in the livelihood they are best suited for and which enables them to obtain the wherewithal they need to support themselves and any family members who are dependent on them.

Changing the way land is owned is simple. Start over. Revoke ownership rights to all land then begin allocating it in order to satisfy all the aspects of life on Earth that require land (i.e., providing societal infrastructure, accommodating residential requirements; and satisfying the land needs of agricultural, industrial, commercial, and recreational endeavors; wildlife; scenic vistas; and forest land preservation, etc.). Once aesthetic land uses have been adequately accommodated, land used for agricultural purposes must be accommodated followed by land for societal infrastructure, residential needs, and recreational facilities then commercial and industrial requirements.

In order to minimize the land allocated to residential and commercial requirements, high-rise structures should be used whenever possible. Every family residence within such structures will be designed to accommodate adequate living quarters, storage for essential implements, and sufficient ground for a garden or recreation area. If a family unit chooses to live off the fruits of its own labor, additional land that enables it to accomplish self-sufficiency will be allocated, but that land may or may not be located adjacent to the family's living quarters. However, it should be located close enough to its living quarters to be easily accessible by a nonpolluting means of transportation, preferably pedestrian or some other form of people-powered conveyance, for example, bicycling.

To ensure that adequate land is allocated for the various purposes listed above, a government agency would have to be responsible for anticipating the needs of Earth's population and managing the Earth's land to ensure that everyone has adequate living accommodations; everyone's means for earning a livelihood is sufficient to sustain a healthy, productive lifestyle and is conveniently accessible; sufficient land is allocated to accommodate societal infrastructure; the land best suited to the harvesting of crops and natural resources is protected; and the associated industrial/distribution infrastructure needed to convert natural resources to necessary products is adequate.

CHAPTER 15

All Biodegradable Trash Must Be Converted to New Uses

Did you know that decaying garbage and ruminating animals produce gas that has the same energy-producing component as the natural gas we extract from beneath the Earth's surface?

Surely, we humans can figure out a way to capture all that gas as it is being produced and use it to maintain the lifestyles to which we've become accustomed. Incidentally, capturing methane gas before it escapes into the atmosphere also helps reduce global warming, because methane gas is one of the most potent greenhouse gases. As it turns out there are already over 425 dumps in the United States that have been rigged to capture methane gas and use it to produce electricity. According to John Donnelly of the *Boston Globe*, almost 800,000 homes in the United States get their electricity from power plants that use methane gas produced by decaying matter in aging landfills across the country. In addition, 1.2 million residences are being heated using landfill-produced gas.

For a garbage dump to produce cost-effective amounts of methane, it must be large, have been in use long enough for its contents to have sufficiently decayed, and have been properly covered in order to restrict exposure to oxygen from the atmosphere. The most effective methane-producing dumps are large landfills that have been filled up and covered over with a layer of soil after a system of intake pipes has been installed so the gas the landfill creates can be collected and put to constructive use.

In the United States, the EPA regulates all landfills and monitors them for release of greenhouse gas into the atmosphere. However, it does not appear that any federal government agency has the responsibility of replacing small municipal dumps with a national network of large regional landfills or establishing an integrated network of processing plants that use the captured methane gas produced by these landfills to supplement the sources of energy presently derived from dwindling underground deposits of oil, natural gas, and coal.

This is an opportunity for citizens throughout the world to mount a coordinated effort to have all biodegradable garbage disposed of in a way that enables the gas produced from its decomposition to be captured and used to slow the depletion of underground natural gas reserves. It is important that such a program be started immediately so that by the time naturally occurring reservoirs of natural gas have been used up, the garbage dump reservoirs will be able to take their place. This will ensure that we will be able to continue using natural gas as an energy source for as long as we continue to produce biodegradable garbage. But the time to act is now, because it takes years for a sealed dump to begin producing gas, and hopefully there's enough natural gas left in underground deposits to last until enough landfills are ready to take over satisfying the demand for this energy source.

SECTION 5

Peaceful Coexistence Is Essential in a Worldwide Community

If history gives any indication of its future, humanity cannot survive within a societal structure that allows individual human beings and independent sovereign nations to put their own interests above the interests of the entire species. This is not a new revelation. In fact, there have been numerous previous attempts to address this problem. Unfortunately, people with attitudes of entitlement and special interests have conspired to prevent any of these attempts from successfully establishing the kind of universal cooperation among all human beings that is necessary to establish lasting peace on Earth. Fortunately, the time has arrived when the world's attention is focused on various attempts to establish personal freedoms in countries where those freedoms have been suppressed by dictatorial regimes. What better time to introduce a universal set of behavioral guidelines that will enable all people to pursue the lifestyle and to adhere to the belief system they choose as long as they are willing to adhere to this universal set of behavioral guidelines in all behavior that involves interacting with other human beings or with any other aspect of Earth's ability to provide a living environment that supports everyone and everything?

CHAPTER 16

Using Self-interest as Motivation for Peaceful Coexistence

All human behavior is motivated by self-interest. In other words, self-interest is what motivates people to do what they do in order to procure the goods and services they need to satisfy their personal needs and desires without expending any more time or effort than is necessary. This attitude is responsible in large part for the problems that threaten chaos for Earth's inhabitants because few seem overly concerned about how their own behavior affects others. This is not a new phenomenon, and over the ages, wise men have attempted to address it by introducing rules and regulations that define the parameters of acceptable behavior and by prescribing penalties intended to dissuade people from intentionally violating those rules and regulations. Unfortunately, these attempts to regulate human behavior have only been partially successful because people are more interested in making their own lives as enjoyable as possible than they are in avoiding behavior that makes the lives of others less enjoyable than would otherwise be possible. If humanity is ever going to overcome the impediment to its survival that self-interest represents, that attitude has to change.

Ironically, appealing to people's self-interest may be the most effective way of getting them to peacefully coexist with one another. If programs were developed to help people understand the benefits of peaceful coexistence, they would be more likely to be receptive to suggestions regarding how modifications in their lifestyle and attitudes of self-interest will result in living conditions that are more enjoyable for them. In other words, the best way to persuade people that peaceful coexistence is worthwhile is to show them why peacefully coexisting with one another is in their own best interest. Consider the following rationale for why peaceful coexistence is a good idea.

The primary challenge facing humanity in its struggle to remain viable on Earth is being able to evolve quickly enough as a species to cope with an ever-changing living environment that is becoming ever more inhospitable for human habitation. The primary causes for Earth becoming less hospitable to human habitation are humanity's mindless consumption of Earth's natural resources and its production of more environmental pollution than Earth is able to accommodate. Therefore, all people must be shown why it is in their best interest for them to discontinue all activities that exacerbate these problems, because restricting consumption of Earth's nonrenewable natural resources and curtailing activities that pollute Earth's living environment enable Earth to continue supporting human life for as long as possible. In addition, people must be shown why propagating the species improves the chances that offspring will be produced that are better equipped to handle an aspect of their living environment that is presently adversely affecting some human beings, perhaps even their own children.

No one in their right mind would intentionally do anything that they know will make it more difficult for their children and their children's children to enjoy their lifetime on Earth, so even the most disconnected societies of human beings are likely to be receptive to ideas that are more likely to ensure that their future generations will thrive. I'd be willing to bet that no individuals who are asked whether they would intentionally engage in behavior that they knew would make life less enjoyable for their own future generations would answer "yes." Unfortunately, there's a disconnect between how people answer that question and the mind-set they have while engaging in the tasks that need to get done in order to attain their chosen lifestyle. Therefore, people have to be shown how alternative ways of accomplishing the same result are not only better for them, but also ensure that their children and their children's children will inherit an Earth that is able to accommodate them as effectively as past generations.

So how can people be made aware that almost everything they do in living their lives contributes to conditions or circumstances that will ultimately affect the health and well-being of their own future generations if not themselves and members of their immediate family and their extended family of friends and acquaintances? The answer depends on how advanced members of a particular society are. For those in advanced societies like the United States, the best way would be for all human beings to become proactive in living their lives in ways that require consumption of as few natural resources as possible and produce as little pollution as possible. They must also become proactive in encouraging others to do likewise.

In order for that to happen, people must not only lead by example, but also they must become activists lobbying to get laws passed that require everyone to accomplish their chosen lifestyle without using up inordinate amounts of non-renewable natural resources or the products made from nonrenewable natural resources. Laws must also require that products no longer be produced if their production or use creates residues that pollute Earth's living environment or impede Earth from being able to continue adequately supporting all its existing life forms.

For those in less advanced societies such as those found in developing countries, which are also known as third world countries, the only way to get human beings to live their lives in ways that require consumption of as few natural resources as possible and produce as little pollution as possible is to initiate missionary programs that send people out to train others in ways to accomplish the tasks essential to life maintenance in ways better for them and for the environment. Such programs could be modeled on the United States' Peace Corps, which has sent over 200,000 people to 139 countries so far. The Peace Corps' objectives are to help set up training programs within target countries that prepare people to train their country's men and women in the use of methods and procedures that will improve their self-sufficiency and improve the connectivity between all the citizens of the countries whose people are being helped and the citizens of the countries that have sent volunteers to help them achieve a higher standard of living.

If all countries in the world that have the wherewithal to do so decided to emulate the Peace Corps model, eventually the inhabitants of all countries on Earth would have learned how to adequately sustain themselves, peacefully coexist with their neighbors, and teach their future generations to do likewise. When that happens, a community of nations of likeminded individuals will have been established thereby accomplishing the necessary prerequisite for establishing Earth as a place where all inhabitants are committed to doing what they can to ensure that Earth's ability to support them and their future generations is not impaired and that every human being on Earth is able to share in Earth's bounty to the extent necessary to sustain a viable, fruitful existence.

CHAPTER 17

Peaceful Coexistence Requires
Universal Rules
for Acceptable Behavior

There are several obstacles impeding the implementation of consistent worldwide expectations regarding acceptable and unacceptable behavior as well as how to encourage the former and discourage the latter. First, there is no consistency in the way the world's children are raised or behavioral attitudes instilled in them by those who raise them. Furthermore, all human beings regard how they raise their children as being their responsibility and nobody else's. They resent advice from others, and others, knowing this, are reluctant to give it. Therefore, this paradigm has to be changed, because the way children behave when they become adults depends in large part on the way they were raised.

If every human being in the world is expected to conform to a worldwide set of expectations regarding acceptable and unacceptable behavior, all persons who are responsible for teaching children how they are to behave must teach them to conform to that set of rules regardless of the religion they practice or the societal traditions prevalent in the place on Earth where they live. In addition, all members of the human race must accept this dichotomy by respecting all people's right to live their life as they please as long as their actions adhere to the same universal rules of behavior to which everyone else is expected to adhere.

Second, it is essential that all people assume the responsibility of not only ensuring their own family's adherence to an established universal set of behavior rules, but also assume responsibility for helping ensure that everyone else is doing likewise. Therefore, whenever a person observes even a stranger behaving in a way that violates these behavioral rules, that person must speak up and point out why the observed behavior violates expectations. A simple reminder should be sufficient to correct an error in judgment. On the other hand, there will be people who intentionally violate the rules, so a means of dealing with them must be developed that doesn't cause a confrontational situation.

In past societies, ostracism has proven to be an effective way of accomplishing that objective, and it could very well be the best way to accomplish the objective in a worldwide community of human beings. In order for such a system to work, everyone must be able to identify everyone else whom they encounter in the course of living their lives. In addition, a universal communication network would have to be established so information about violations of the rules for acceptable behavior could be broadcast to all participants. This is necessary in order to keep everyone informed of all occurrences of people intentionally violating behavioral rules and refusing to acknowledge their wrongdoing. When the violator's identity is known to the witness or witnesses, names and places of residence should be included in the information provided. If the observed violation involves a stranger or strangers, witnesses must try to identify the violator or violators using other means. For example, if they can, they should write down a license plate number if a vehicle was being used. They should also jot down a physical description of those involved in as much detail as possible. Obviously, taking a photo with a smart phone or some other picture-taking device is preferable.

Ensuring that all people adhere to the same set of rules for acceptable behavior requires everyone's involvement. Involvement entails letting one's own behavior set a good example, and it involves being forthcoming in taking others to task when their behavior violates the rules for acceptable behavior. This is essential, because until everyone adheres to the same rules for acceptable behavior, there is little likelihood that an attitude of community will take root. When residents in every neighborhood become proactive in getting to know everyone else in their neighborhood, violators of behavioral rules are more likely to be receptive to efforts by neighbors who attempt to correct unacceptable behavior. Therefore, everyone in a neighborhood must take the time to visit with their neighbors whenever the opportunity to do so presents itself, and they must faithfully attend regularly scheduled neighborhood meetings intended to discuss problems and to introduce new residents in the neighborhood.

Sadly, in most communities, individuals don't take the time to be personally involved in meeting new residents or in ensuring that everyone they encounter adheres to the established rules for behavior. They prefer to hire others to do that for them, because they fear the possibility of an unpleasant interaction or retribution. On the other hand, if everyone within the community is willing to get involved in calling out a violator of acceptable behavior, the fear of retribution diminishes exponentially. The point is, when observed behavior is not criminal but does violate acceptable societal expectations, all people who are members of that community must personally express their disapproval. Furthermore, when commendable behavior is observed, such behavior must be brought to everyone's attention and the persons involved must be encouraged to do more of the same. Otherwise, a sense of community is not likely to ever develop either within a neighborhood or worldwide.

CHAPTER 18

Introducing the Concepts of the Basic Precept and Mutual Empathy

Human creativity is lost when individuality is suppressed by laws that restrict people's freedom to express themselves verbally and via written word or by some other form of artistic expression. There are plenty of examples in human history where authoritarian governments tried to do just that and were forced to give their citizens back those freedoms to avoid or end revolutions and remain a viable influence in the governance of their country. Nevertheless, some of Earth's citizens are still being subjected to authoritarianism, and that will likely continue to be the case until the time arrives when every human being has learned to adhere to the following basic precept:

"Be all you can be and do all you can do as long as what you choose to be and what you choose to do isn't harmful to yourself or to others or to anything else that exists on Earth, and you don't prevent anyone or anything else from doing likewise. In addition, trust that every other person will behave in like manner."

If every human being is precious as stated in chapter 3, then all human beings must adopt the attitude that as long as individuals are not doing anything that physically threatens their own well-being or the well-being of anything or anyone else, that individual should be allowed to live their life however he or she pleases. It shouldn't matter what religion a person practices or whether he or she practices any religion. Religions are simply a means for teaching people how to treat one another, and as long as people learn to adhere to the aforementioned basic precept in all that they do, the religious rituals they choose to practice are a matter of personal preference. The important thing is for all people to learn to respect and care for themselves as well as everyone and everything else they affect in the course of living their lives, because the well-being of all life on Earth depends on the success of the symbiotic relationships every individual organism has with every other organism upon which it relies in order to thrive.

Since all human beings are precious, no one can afford to discount the value of one's own or anybody else's life. In other words, all human beings must learn to practice mutual empathy in all interactions with all life forms on Earth, because mutual empathy is the behavioral attitude that every human being must have toward all other human beings and all other life forms on Earth to properly adhere to the basic precept. So what is mutual empathy? It is what motivates individuals to help each other because they are part of a group of individuals who have something in common. Mutual empathy is common among those who are associated with one another as the result of being a family member or a team member or because of their association with others who have joined together to accomplish a common goal. It's also what motivates a person to come to the aid of a complete stranger who appears to be in need.

In a society in which all persons have not learned to be mutually empathetic and to practice the basic precept, there may be some trepidation about coming to the assistance of a complete stranger, particularly when the person in need is different in a way that causes the potential "Good Samaritan" to experience trepidation due to an ingrained societal prejudice. But a world community atti-tude can never come to fruition unless people decide to ignore such trepidations and decide that all human beings deserve to be treated with mutual empathy and according to the basic precept. On the bright side, when people witness how people respond to persons who practice mutual empathy and the basic precept, they are influenced to emulate that behavior in order to elicit the same response. This is why the practice of mutual empathy and the basic precept has the poten-tial to affect the way people interact with other people regardless of how well they know them. People will begin to regard all the other people living on Earth as deserving of the same compassion and consideration they have for the people with whom they are personally acquainted and with whom they interact regu-larly. And when that happens, a sense of community will begin to develop among all human beings living on Earth.

Practicing the basic precept and mutual empathy will also influence people to be concerned about how their behavior impacts Earth's ability to support life.

For example, on Earth, structures such as rocks, soil, water, and all living things are the result of chemical combinations among Earth's various elements. The elements are indivisible, but the structures they build are not. Consequently, as soon as an organic or inorganic structure is created and it begins to interact with the environment in which it exists, it becomes susceptible to transformation or degradation as it encounters elements in that environment that affect its chemical composition.

Since humans are an amalgamation of structures created from Earth's elements, they are susceptible to changes in their living environment that impact the process of creating and sustaining their bodies. Therefore, they have a vested interest in protecting and preserving the process by which they are created and sustained. That's where the basic precept and mutual empathy come in. They are the influences that cause a person to consider whether a contemplated action will have good consequences or bad, and they engender the inclination to avoid taking any action that may have a bad consequence even when the apparent result is personal gratification. Put another way, the basic precept and mutual empathy help human beings avoid taking contemplated actions when they sense that the result of those actions will endanger them or others or some aspect of creation upon which the human species depends for its survival.

CHAPTER 19

Integrating the Basic Precept and Mutual Empathy into Lifestyles

The following paragraphs describe how mutual empathy and the basic precept influence various kinds of human behavior to be positive and constructive rather than negative and destructive.

MODERATING COMPETITIVE INSTINCTS AND CREATIVITY

The basic precept and mutual empathy are essential in moderating the human need for gratification. These influences are what will ensure that the creative response to circumstances that stimulate action or reaction is constructive rather than destructive or counterproductive. In competitive situations, they keep competitors from being tempted to bend the rules to gain an advantage. On the other hand, they also keep superior competitors from saying anything or acting in any way that would belittle opponents' abilities or distract them from doing their best. Instead, they are what make the winners want to sincerely congratulate the losers for their competitiveness and to encourage them to keep competing, because, as the old saying goes, it's not whether you win or lose, but how you play the game.

CONTROLLING SEXUAL IMPULSE

The basic precept and mutual empathy also influence the way humans behave when they are sexually aroused. They don't change your sexuality or your sexual desire. Those are natural aspects of human nature. They simply influence behavior when sexual arousal occurs and it isn't mutual, or it is mutual but other circumstances make it imprudent to pursue intercourse because doing so will have a harmful effect on either or both participants or on others who are related to one of the participants in an intimate way. In other words, the basic precept and mutual empathy enable anyone who becomes sexually attracted to someone else to resist pursuing a sexual relationship if doing so is likely to have adverse repercussions. After all, the whole objective of sex is to bring two people together to experience all the aspects of living that create happiness and satisfaction ranging from sustaining and nurturing one another to creating, sustaining, and nurturing children.

In other words, the basic precept and mutual empathy influence unattached individuals to avoid having intercourse simply to satisfy their sexual appetites, because both participants in these circumstances will know that sexual intercourse between two humans is completely satisfying only when both participants get back as much as they give. That doesn't happen when sexual intercourse is forced by one participant on the other. In fact, the more likely outcome in that instance is that one or both of the participants will feel unfulfilled and used, in which case, instead of being the catalyst that transforms a relationship into a long-lasting, fulfilling experience, sexual intercourse becomes a detrimental influence that threatens to undermine the relationship and cause psychological damage.

Masturbation can also have detrimental consequences on a couple's intimacy if the person doing it is involved in a committed relationship. That's because self-stimulation can rob a relationship of its spontaneity, and spontaneity is one of the most wonderful aspects of a couple's sexual interaction. Worse yet, self-stimulation may affect one partner's willingness to respond to the needs of the other and that can have a negative impact on this aspect of their relationship. On the other hand, it is a way to relieve sexual tension when sexual intercourse is not a prudent option.

CONTROLLING CAUSES OF DISEASE

The basic precept and mutual empathy also play a role in humans' efforts to deal with those aspects of their living environment that cause disease or some other physiological problem. Certain funguses and bacteria as well as numerous viruses threaten humanity's health because some aspect of these organisms' life cycles causes disease in the human body, and even though humans have discovered ways to defend themselves against the effect these pathogens have on their physiology, they've eliminated few, if any, from continuing to be a threat. Consequently, humanity is at risk of being overcome by one or more of these microorganisms unless it learns how to speed up its own adaptation process.

In order to speed up their adaptation process, humans must learn to manage their reproduction so that when a chance variation in a person's genetic material enables that person's body to resist a known pathogen or become more physiologically adept, that variation can be identified and introduced into all succeeding offspring of all members of the species so that everyone born afterward will be more disease resistant and more physiologically sound.

Each species perpetuates itself through reproduction, and it adapts to changes in its living environment that threaten its viability through genetic mutation. Reproduction occurs when the genetic material from a male and a female combine to produce offspring. Genetic mutations occur when the resulting combination of genetic material creates an offspring whose bodily characteristics include a physical characteristic or functional capability that wasn't present in either of its progenitors. Such variations are the best way an organism has of adapting to changes in its living environment or resisting invasion by microorganisms that threaten its well-being.

Once a variation occurs, it is very likely that the individual who has it will pass it on to its progeny, but it only gets passed to that individual's next generation, not every new individual of the species, so it takes a very long time for a new characteristic to manifest itself throughout a species or subspecies. That's because that only happens if the new characteristic bestows some advantage on those who have it that enables them to be more likely to survive and successfully reproduce in their living environment than those who don't have it.

In chapter 10, ways that enable humans to manage their own genetic improvements were discussed. By keeping physiological records on individuals from their birth to their death, an analysis could be made of all humans' responses to the health-threatening events that occurred during their lifetime in the places where they lived. This would allow researchers to identify all individuals who have a genetic variation that allows them to be more physiologically successful than contemporaries at tolerating the environmental influences to which they are exposed in the place on Earth where they live. As explained in chapter 10, the ability to analyze the genetic makeup of such individuals would enable researchers to identify anomalies that could then be used to help all humans become impervious to adverse environmental influences. Such procedures, when coupled with the continued development of medicines, will improve humanity's ability to maintain its viability on Earth and beyond.

Of course, it is imperative that the basic precept and mutual empathy influence those who engage in these procedures so that they are able to resist the temptation of using genetic manipulation as a tool to create an unfair advantage for themselves. In other words, the basic precept and mutual empathy are the influences that make everyone want to do what's best for the whole species, and that is essential if the human species is ever going to coalesce into a cohesive society that includes all human beings living on Earth.

CURTAILING RESOURCE DEPLETION

When humans learn to use the basic precept and mutual empathy to influence their behavior, they'll become more sensitive to how their chosen lifestyle affects creation's ability to continue supporting life on Earth. And, they'll be more willing to change those aspects of their lifestyle that impair Earth's ability to maintain the living environment their well-being requires. That's because they'll understand that every moment of their life, every action they take depletes some of Earth's natural resources, and those natural resources may or may not be replaceable.

It's time for a paradigm shift. All people need to learn to use the basic precept and mutual empathy to guide their decision-making process. This is particularly true when it pertains to their attitudes regarding durable goods. Everyone must be willing to limit themselves to an adequate wardrobe as well as one dwelling, one mode of transportation, and one each of the various other implements needed to facilitate a healthy and productive lifestyle. Furthermore, everyone should insist that all applicable products be as nonpolluting and energy efficient as is technologically possible. As stated previously, limiting consumption of durable goods reduces consumption of natural resources and prolongs the availability of those resources that are essential to human viability. Furthermore, limiting pollution and improving energy efficiency not only conserves natural resources, but also improves Earth's effectiveness in providing a healthy living environment.

The basic precept and mutual empathy will also influence people to consume only nutritious food and only in amounts sufficient to maintain their bodies in their optimum functional condition. Furthermore, the basic precept and mutual empathy will motivate people to exercise their bodies to whatever extent is necessary to maintain muscle and bone functionality as well as weight and physique in order to minimize the need to replace clothes that no longer fit due to weight gain or loss. Of course, as explained previously, there are natural changes in body shape and size throughout each person's lifetime, so an exchange procedure would be essential in order to accommodate these kinds of changes without necessitating the creation of new clothing unless there is a shortage of comparable garments in the size needed.

Since natural resources are consumed when any kind of implement is made or clothing is created or shelter is constructed, it is essential that whatever is made from natural resources be created and maintained in a way that enables that product to remain functional indefinitely unless further use is impractical. When further use becomes impractical, these kinds of durable products must be recycled so residual resources can be reclaimed and put to other uses.

Consider how humans typically dispose of biodegradable garbage. Most of it is dumped into landfills where it decomposes in a limited oxygen environment. The result is ground water pollution from run-off and the production of methane and other greenhouse gasses from organic material decomposition. Since this kind of methane gas has the same energy-producing component as the natural gas obtained from underground wells, it is reusable as a source of energy. However, if it and other gasses are allowed to escape from landfills and enter the atmosphere they exacerbate global warming. To keep that from happening, biodegradable garbage must be disposed of in a way that prevents production of methane gas and salvages any beneficial byproducts that decomposition produces without polluting ground water, or it should be disposed of in a way that prevents ground water pollution and enables the reclamation of all reusable materials including methane gas.

To summarize, the basic precept and mutual empathy influence us to choose the best course of action in all that we do so that the outcome achieved is best for every aspect of creation on Earth affected by the alternatives being considered. It is essential that we use both when making decisions regarding our use of durable goods to make our lives more productive and enjoyable, because all durable goods are created from natural resources, and Earth has limited amounts of natural resources.

CURTAILING EXPEDIENT INVENTION

Humans have a tendency to invent tools and practices expediently. The basic precept and mutual empathy influence people to consider all the ramifications of a contemplated action before they act and to act only if the anticipated result is what's best for everyone and everything affected by the action being contemplated. When inventors begin to focus on solutions that do not cause harm to any aspect of creation on Earth, Earth will become a healthier, more enjoyable place to live.

ALLOCATING LAND EQUITABLY

The basic precept and mutual empathy should influence people to respect the fact that Earth and its resources belong to everyone and that everyone should benefit equitably. In other words, the benefits derived from Earth's land and its resources should accrue to everyone on an equal basis. Therefore, the land and the resources produced from it must be allocated in a way that enables everyone to sustain a viable existence.

In most places, whoever owns a piece of land also owns the rights to whatever natural resources that land contains and is entitled to all the benefits those natural resources produce. Unless everyone becomes more mutually empathetic toward everyone else, taking those benefits away from the few and sharing them with everyone will certainly result in strong objections from those who have to give up their exclusive rights. However, in order for everyone to benefit equally from the use of Earth's land and its natural resources, everyone should be able to occupy enough land to accommodate a homestead, but that right would only apply to the surface of the land on which the improvements are constructed. The area underneath the surface will belong to all humanity and any valuable natural resources contained beneath the surface will be used in a way that benefits all people equitably.

CREATING A UNIVERSAL ATTITUDE OF RESPONSIBILITY AND COMMITMENT

When people learn to use the basic precept and mutual empathy to influence every decision they make, a universal attitude of responsibility and commitment will develop, because the basic precept and mutual empathy will influence how all human beings treat one another. The problem is in finding a way to introduce these concepts and persuade people to use them instead of letting their egos and their attitudes of entitlement motivate their behavior.

The first step is to educate people about why behavior motivated by the basic precept and mutual empathy will ultimately lead to a more satisfactory result than their present way of living. Then, when enough people have accepted that it does, they will begin to influence others to interact with one another and with the rest of creation in a similar way instead of continuing to let their ego and their attitude of entitlement influence their behavior.

Eventually, most people will stop mistreating other people who are not like them, and they'll be more concerned with how the products and procedures they use in the course of daily living impact the environment and human ecology. They'll begin to support business, governmental, and religious leaders whose decisions reflect mutual empathy and the basic precept, and oppose those whose actions and decisions are not influenced by mutual empathy and the basic precept. In other words, when the people choose to let the basic precept and mutual empathy influence all their thoughts and actions, the basic precept and mutual empathy will begin to influence the way businesses, religions, and nations on Earth conduct themselves. As a result, a sense of community will begin to emerge that encompasses all individuals, businesses, religions, and nations on Earth. Eventually, the interests of the whole will supersede the interests of individuals, businesses, nations, and religions, but the diversity of religious and social custom as well as national, group, and individual freedom of expression will be respected, initiative and creativity will continue to be rewarded, and all people will be able to support themselves in a fruitful and fulfilling existence.

In order to get people to be more responsible regarding the consequences of the lifestyle they choose to pursue, they must be taught to practice the basic precept and to be mutually empathetic. In other words, they must be taught to be more aware of the way their behavior affects others and the living environment on which their very existence depends, and they must be taught ways of doing things that accomplish the objective of living healthy, enjoyable lives without resorting to behavior that is detrimental to themselves, others, or some other aspect of the ecological environment on which they depend. When that happens, people will stop mistreating other people who are not like them, and they'll be more concerned with how the products and procedures they use in the course of daily living impact the environment. They'll begin to support business, government, and religious leaders whose decisions reflect mutual empathy and the practice of the basic precept, and they will oppose those whose actions and decisions are not influenced by the basic precept and mutual empathy.

PART II
Considerations Regarding Converting Earth into a World Community

SECTION 1
Adopting Attitudes That Make World Community Possible

The following chapters introduce movements and programs that are considered necessary in order to replace selfishness with inclusiveness, because an attitude of inclusiveness that encompasses all human beings on Earth is a necessary prerequisite to establishing a worldwide community of all human beings living on Earth.

When enough people on Earth have eliminated behavior that adversely affects some aspect of the way Earth and its inhabitants function, and when they have learned to peacefully coexist with one another, Earth will become a much more enjoyable place to live. In order for this to happen, however, everyone will have to eliminate selfishness when deciding which course of action is best for all members of the human race.

Plenty of people have great ideas about how to make Earth a better place, but those ideas have always required concessions from people who will have to change the way they do things in order to comply, and there will always be people who aren't willing to do that. As a result, stalemates result and compromises have to be made in order to get anything done. Unfortunately, compromises usually mean that the problem someone is trying to solve by introducing a better way of doing things ends up being less effective than it needs to be.

It's time for the majority of people on Earth to realize that a very small minority of people control the way things are done on Earth and that these people want things done the way that results in the most benefits for them. They've gotten away with this ploy because the majority of people can't be bothered to make sure every decision made and action taken serves everyone's best interest rather than the special interests of small groups who are trying to protect an advantage they want just for themselves. These attitudes have to change if world community is ever going become a reality.

CHAPTER 20

Using Love to Encourage Acceptable Behavior

Chapter 8 discusses why parents must learn how to use love to teach their children how to behave properly. In order to love one another, people must learn to be mutually empathetic with all other human beings they encounter in the course of their lifetimes. In other words, mutual empathy is the attitude that all individual human beings must have toward all other human beings to ensure that every human being's existence is adequately sustained and that he or she is able to pursue a healthy, fruitful lifestyle. That's because mutual empathy is what motivates individuals to help each other regardless of the status of their relationship. It's what motivates people to apply the basic precept in all interactions with other people.

When people are family members or team members, or are part of a group of nonrelated individuals who have joined together to accomplish a common goal, mutual empathy comes naturally, because when these kinds of groups practice mutual empathy, they are more likely to thrive and succeed than would otherwise be the case. When people within groups are looking out for themselves primarily, they're not that concerned about the feelings and well-being of every other person within the group. When a group is large, there is likely to be less intimacy among all members of the group, and that makes it less likely that all individuals within the group will experience mutual empathy with all members of the larger group. Consequently, the challenge is to convince all people that their attitudes and behaviors toward everyone they encounter should be the same as their behaviors and attitudes toward their family and close friends, because, from the point of view of humanity's well-being, every human being living on Earth is equally important and deserves to be regarded with mutual empathy. If all people were to become mutually empathetic with everyone in the world they encounter, and they used the basic precept as the attitudinal influence governing the way they interact with others, a world community attitude would quickly become a reality.

Unfortunately, the prevalent attitude people have toward people with whom they have not been acquainted is indifference, so why would anyone who derives any kind of advantage from the way things are done presently willingly change their attitude toward people they don't know or care about? Why should they make sure their interactions with everyone and everything they encounter enable all human beings to achieve a fruitful, fulfilling existence?

The answer is self-interest. The health and well-being of individuals depends on the success of their interactions not only with their own kind, but also with all the other organisms upon which their well-being depends. In other words, symbiosis is essential to life on Earth, and humanity must learn to avoid all behavior that adversely alters any symbiotic relationship essential to its ability to flourish on Earth. Therefore, all human beings must be encouraged to pursue only those lifestyles that produce health, well-being, and contentment without having to engage in behavior that prevents anyone or anything else from being able to do likewise.

When all people commit to doing that, they will tend to adopt ways of doing things that enable them to live healthy, enjoyable lives without having to resort to behavior that is detrimental to themselves or to others or to some other aspect of the ecological environment on which they depend. In other words, people will begin to avoid letting ego and self-interest dictate their behavior, and the result will be that their interactions with one another and with the rest of creation will be supportive and constructive rather than hurtful and destructive. As a result, people will be less likely to mistreat others who are dissimilar to themselves and more likely to be concerned with how the products and procedures they use in the course of daily living impact their own as well as everyone else's living environment. In addition, they'll be more likely to support individuals, businesses, governmental officials, and religious leaders whose behavior and decision making is influenced by the basic precept and mutual empathy and less likely to support those whose behavior and decision making is not influenced by the basic precept and mutual empathy.

In summary, when people choose to let the basic precept and mutual empathy influence all their thoughts and actions, all individuals, businesses, religions, and nations on Earth will begin to conduct themselves in a way that enables a sense of community to develop that encompasses all individuals, businesses, and nations on Earth. That's because individuals, businesses, nations, and religions will begin to put the interests of humanity ahead of their own, and while the diversity of religious and social customs as well as national, group, and individual freedom of expression will be respected and initiative and creativity will continue to be rewarded, the freedom to experience a fruitful and fulfilling existence will become equally available to every human being living on Earth.

CHAPTER 21
Eliminating Problems Caused by Humanity's Behavioral Evolution

Previous chapters have discussed ways in which human behavior has impeded humanity from reaching the point in its behavioral evolution where all human beings have accepted that every member of the human species has a role in helping our species continue its evolution. Other chapters have focused on the attitudes that humanity must cultivate in order to enable it to coalesce into a cohesive, worldwide community of individuals who are willing to modify the manner in which they attain what they need to satisfy their personal needs and to eliminate behavior that prevents other human beings from being able to do likewise.

As mentioned previously, in the book entitled *The Science Of Good & Evil*, Michael Shermer claims that disparate groups, who might otherwise go to war with one another because one group has something the other group needs or simply wants, will tend to peacefully coexist if they learn how to trade amongst themselves to obtain what they need or want rather than take it by force or by stealth. What if all human beings on Earth could learn to share Earth's natural resources equitably? The world would become a worldwide community of human beings in which all people are able to sustain themselves in a viable existence and no one would suffer deprivation. The challenge is figuring out how to teach all humans the right way to convert natural resources into useful products and distribute those products so that all human beings are able to obtain what they need to sustain a healthy, productive lifestyle

Since the Earth's resources are not evenly distributed, some areas have an abundance of natural resources and other areas have few natural resources. In some cases, these natural resources are the ingredients for food, manufactured goods, and building materials. In other cases, the natural resources involve sources of energy and potable water. As things are today, given the present geopolitical structure, people who live in countries that have few natural resources are more likely to face deprivation than those who live in countries that have abundant natural resources.

But deprivation can also be the result of the way resources are owned and distributed even in countries that have abundant natural resources. Consequently, the way natural resources are owned and distributed needs to be changed. Exclusive rights to the Earth's natural resources that happen to be on or under land claimed by a private individual or a sovereign nation must be revoked and those rights must become the property of all inhabitants of planet Earth. Furthermore, the expectation must be established that all Earth's resources will be utilized in the way that benefits all Earth's inhabitants equitably.

In times past, the nation with the greatest military strength felt free to claim whatever natural resources its people desired, and the people did so without concern for the deprivation such actions might cause the residents of areas where the desired natural resources were located. Today, that attitude still exists, but it's no longer sovereign nations that are responsible for hoarding natural resources—it is corporate conglomerates operating under the protection of sovereign governments. Either way, the bottom line is still the same. Residents in areas where natural resources exist do not necessarily benefit from the extraction of those natural resources, at least not to the same extent as those who are associated with the conglomerate doing the extraction and those who are fortunate enough to own the mineral rights for the land where extractions take place.

Why should luck and force determine who benefits from natural resource extraction and who doesn't? It shouldn't. In fact, all of Earth's natural resources belong to all human beings and should be used to ensure that all human beings living on Earth as well as all other life forms on which human survival depends have enough of Earth's natural resources and the produce of those natural resources to sustain their viability.

So how can we ensure that everyone and everything has what is needed to sustain healthy, productive existences? Since human beings have an innate mutual empathy for one another, they have the capacity for caring about the well-being and happiness of other human beings, even human beings with whom they have no personal relationship. Therefore, it is time for all human beings to enable their mutual empathy and accept that every individual member of their species deserves to be allowed to adequately sustain themselves. Otherwise, they may not get the opportunity to contribute whatever they can toward improving the quality of humanity's existence, be it a genetic mutation, or a revolutionary idea, or simply a conduit that enables the next generation of human beings to exist.

It is imperative that humanity institutes the changes needed to ensure that everyone on Earth shares Earth's resources more efficiency and effectively; all human beings are able to live healthy, productive lives; and Earth is able to continue providing an unimpaired, healthy, supportive living environment for as long a period of time as possible. Furthermore, each of us must adopt the attitude that as long as individuals are not doing anything that physically threatens their own well-being or the well-being of anything or anyone else, they should be allowed to live their life however he or she pleases. It shouldn't matter what religion a person practices or that the person does not practice a religion. Religion is simply a means of teaching people how to treat one another, and when people have mutual empathy for one another and practice the basic precept in all that they do, the religious rituals they practice are a matter of personal preference.

The important thing is for all people to learn to respect and care for themselves as well as everyone and everything else they affect in the course of living their lives. After all, the well-being of all life on Earth depends on the success of the symbiotic relationships every individual organism has with every other organism on which it relies in order to thrive.

In order to accomplish enabling every human being to live a healthy, productive life, all sovereign nations must willingly give up any claims that impede these objectives from being accomplished and they must join with all other nations to form a world community of all human beings in which everyone is committed to using the basic precept and mutual empathy as guidelines for acceptable behavior. This is necessary in order to ensure that regardless of where on Earth a person lives, that person's behavior will conform to a universal set of behavioral guidelines based on the basic precept, and that he or she will refrain from consuming any more of Earth's natural resources than is necessary to sustain a universally accepted standard of living.

The transition from the world's current geopolitical arrangement to a world community of all human beings will require that all sovereign forms of government adopt rules for behavior that conform to these objectives. They must also implement the necessary infrastructure to ensure that every man, woman, and child living within their jurisdiction is able to live peacefully and has what the person needs to sustain a universally accepted standard of living. This will require ensuring that no one engages in a lifestyle that is deemed to be excessive. Furthermore, an overriding governmental entity must be established to ensure that all sovereign forms of government are treating their citizens and visitors in an equitable manner by taking corrective action to eliminate inequities wherever they are found to exist.

CHAPTER 22

Adopt Behavioral Attitudes Essential in a World Community

The following is a catalog of behavioral attitudes that all human beings must adopt in order to create the cohesiveness that will create a worldwide feeling of community among all human beings living on Earth.

EVERYONE MUST LEARN HOW TO BE CIVIL TO AND CONSIDERATE OF OTHERS

What does being civil and considerate entail? According to *The Oxford American College Dictionary*, being civil is defined as being courteous and polite. Being courteous is defined as being polite, respectful, or considerate in manner. Being polite is defined as having or showing respectful and considerate behavior. Being respectful is defined as having due regard for the feelings, wishes, rights, or traditions of others. Being considerate is defined as being careful not to cause inconvenience or hurt to others. Therefore I have deduced that if *The Oxford American College Dictionary* had an entry for the phrase "being civil and considerate", it would likely be defined as having due regard for the feelings, wishes, rights and traditions of others while taking care not to cause anyone inconvenience or hurt.

CONSUMERS MUST MODERATE THEIR CONSUMPTION OF NEW PRODUCTS

Humans must learn to resist the inclination to acquire new things every time a manufacturer advertises something new and improved or more appealing. They must eliminate the unnecessary consumption of goods in order to always be on the cutting edge of what's new. In other words, people must learn to not let consumerism overwhelm pragmatism as they are being constantly bombarded with advertisements enticing them to abandon functional and useful items for something else that serves the same purpose. To do that, consumers need to change their ideas of what justifies a legitimate need to discard something they already own or to replace it with something else.

Clothing, utensils, and modes of transportation are all means for making our lives more effective and enjoyable, but their manufacture requires depletion of natural resources and Earth's natural resources are not limitless. Therefore, we all must be ever mindful that we owe it to our future generations to moderate the amount of durable goods we consume during our lifetime so there will continue to be natural resources available to produce the items they'll need during their lifetimes. That means we should all adopt the mind-set that as long as a durable item continues to serve its purpose, we must properly maintain it and continue using it until it reaches the point at which further use is no longer possible.

On the other hand, it behooves us to replace automated products that depend on nonrenewable natural resources to make them work when significant improvements have been developed that reduce the amount of natural resources consumed to make them work. Fortunately, this conundrum can be solved by using modularization to enable improvements without having to replace the whole product. If NASA can do it with its space rockets, surely others can do so for more mundane things like automobiles and other durable goods that can be modularized.

The point is, in today's more affluent societies, advertisers are incessantly encouraging people to buy replacements for items they already own because the replacements are alleged to be more effective at attracting attention, more in vogue, more efficient, better for the environment, etc. As previously stated, improvements in product efficiency, durability, and effectiveness are necessary goals as is pollution reduction. But cultivating a mind-set that buying new things is essential to establishing a desirable persona obviates natural resource conservation.

Therefore, manufacturers need to change their mind-set from having to produce new durable products when justifiable improvements are made to producing modularized products that can be updated without having to replace the whole product by simply replacing obsolete components with ones that improve performance. In other words, the objective of manufacturing should be to design and produce products that perform the desired task and can be updated one component at a time as significant improvements are made. This will reduce the need to replace multicomponent end products with new ones every time improvements are made.

On the other hand, durable products like automobiles are usually traded in when they are replaced, and that's okay because, unless the vehicle being traded in is no longer capable of being resold, it is sold to someone who cannot afford to buy new. On the other hand, clothing and lesser appliances and implements that are commonly acquired to make life easier or more enjoyable can't be traded in. Consequently, people dispose of them some other way. One option is to donate unwanted items to places like Goodwill Industries, The Salvation Army, or some other charitable organization that then distributes them to people who are down on their luck. Another alternative is to have a garage sale, and the beauty of that option is that it allows sellers to recoup at least some of the money that they spent when purchasing the items. Finally, if durable items are no longer useful to anyone, they can be recycled, and there are plenty of enterprises that'll take whatever you wish to discard and, depending on the kinds of materials involved, some will even pay you a little money for the things they accept.

Throwing durable products away is not an option. As discussed elsewhere, all that does is fill up waste dump sites with materials that do not decompose quickly and may produce pollution problems. Furthermore, it prevents any recoverable materials from being put to another use thereby reducing the depletion of natural resources.

PEOPLE MUST MODERATE EXPEDIENT BEHAVIOR

Chapters 5 and 19 present reasons why people engage in expedient behavior. When time is of the essence, people take shortcuts and when they do, the effectiveness of the end result may be compromised. Consider the race to send men to the moon and back. The United States and the USSR were competing to be the first to send men to the moon and return them safely back to Earth. Such a complex mission required extraordinary discipline in making sure that the objective could be accomplished successfully without compromising the safety of the participants.

Obviously, in such a complex mission involving incredibly complex instrumentation and extremely small margins for error, an extraordinary amount of attention to every detail is essential. On the other hand, it was also essential to accomplish the task before the competitor did. As history shows, the U.S. effort was successful and space flight stands as one of the most successful and historic of human endeavors.

On the other hand, there are plenty of examples of attempts to accomplish something that had never been accomplished that ended up a failure because someone failed to anticipate all the eventualities or took a shortcut in the interest of saving time. But even when a space mission experienced problems and the mission was in peril, all was not lost because people took the time to figure out what had to be done to save the day, checked to ensure their calculations were correct then resolutely implemented the necessary corrective measures.

The point is, when an action is expedited, there is a risk that some detail will be overlooked that imperils the outcome. Therefore, while time may be of the essence, enough of it must always be taken to ensure that the desired outcome is the one most likely to occur.

EVERY FAMILY MEMBER MUST HELP WITH HOUSEHOLD CHORES

All people who are mature enough to be held responsible for their actions should be taught to engage in activities that enable all the members of their family to sustain an acceptable lifestyle. Those activities may involve earning the wherewithal to sustain a family unit or it may involve performing housekeeping chores that help their family unit to function effectively. In other words, all members of a family unit should be required to do whatever work they can to help the family unit function as effectively as possible.

Typically, household responsibilities include maintaining the family's dwelling, the various tools, and implements that household maintenance requires, and the clothing and other durable goods that family members use to accomplish their household tasks effectively. It should also include the expectation that while a person lives in one's parents' or guardians' home, all members of the household including children will avoid doing anything that increases the time it takes to keep their house and its contents clean, well maintained and tidy. Unfortunately, most family units exempt young children from this responsibility, but including them teaches them to take responsibility for their behavior early on, which helps them develop into more responsible adults.

PEOPLE'S ATTITUDES REGARDING DURABLE GOODS MUST CHANGE

Each family unit should be permitted to accumulate a collection of durable goods sufficient to accommodate the needs of all family members, be it a means of transportation, the various tools and implements required to accomplish the tasks associated with homemaking, or the family's accumulated collection of clothing used to accommodate the inevitable changes in physique as children grow from babies to adults and as adults' physiques change due to overeating or dieting or changes in physical exercise. In other words, for things like clothes and cooking utensils, nothing should be discarded. Instead, such items should be kept and properly maintained until it becomes evident that further use by family members is highly unlikely. Then such items should be turned in if they are reusable. Otherwise, they should be recycled so reusable raw materials can be reclaimed.

EVERYONE MUST ENGAGE IN WORK THAT HELPS ONE'S FAMILY UNIT FUNCTION EFFECTIVELY

In some family units, people prefer to pursue a livelihood that enables them to hire outsiders to provide all necessary support services required to sustain the household. Other family units choose to use only those support services that free up the time needed to properly nurture their young children during their early years. What is not acceptable is for people to fill their time with activities that neither contribute to the effective functioning of a family unit, nor contribute by helping earn the wherewithal required to effectively sustain their household.

THOSE THAT CAN AFFORD TO, MUST HELP THOSE WHO ARE UNABLE TO HELP THEMSELVES

Since the great majority of people living on Earth today struggle to eke out a living sufficient enough to adequately support themselves and their families, they are faced with a different set of problems. A lot of people on Earth have insufficient land to grow what they need to sustain themselves and they live in places where no work is available that would enable them to earn enough to adequately support themselves and their families. When a person is denied an opportunity to earn the means to achieve an adequate standard of living, that person has few options for ensuring his or her survival other than scavenging, begging, stealing, or prostituting.

There should be a universal expectation that all individuals who can afford to do so will contribute what they can to help the less fortunate obtain the testing and training needed to enable them to do the work best suited to their mental and physical abilities. Furthermore, all land on Earth must be reallocated so everyone's need for housing is accommodated. Afterward, the remaining land must be allocated to accommodate adequate governmental and economic infrastructure as well as the agricultural, recreational, educational, and leisure activities required to support all human beings.

People who choose not to live off the land they own will be required to relinquish control of land in excess of that which accommodates all the members of their family unit. Excess land and improvements must be liquidated so that those who don't have a place of residence can be accommodated.

ESTABLISH A WORLDWIDE GOVERNING ENTITY TO FACILITATE A WORLD COMMUNITY ATTITUDE

In order to create the cohesiveness that will create a worldwide feeling of community among all human beings living on Earth, it will be necessary to establish an overriding governmental agency that will be responsible for anticipating the needs of Earth's human population and for managing economic activity worldwide. This will ensure that everyone is able to sustain a healthy, productive lifestyle and that all the services they require to assist them in attaining that objective are available to them. This means that nations as they exist today will no longer have sovereignty over the land within their jurisdiction. Their scope of operation will be limited to the task of ensuring the well-being of the citizens living within their jurisdiction. All decisions regarding the disposition of natural resources and the conversion of natural resources into products will be made by a department of the overriding governmental agency.

CHAPTER 23

Require All Persons Raising a Child to Follow Acceptable Practices

All parents must be taught the most effective ways to help their children develop the kind of character they'll need to be viable members of society. To do that, parents will have to learn to interact with their children using the basic precept. That means, parents must be taught a way of interacting with their children that may differ from the way their parents, or whoever raised them, treated them. In order to do that, all people will have to learn how to be mutually empathetic, and they will have to be trained in how to apply the basic precept when interacting with their children as well as with everyone else. This will help ensure that the way people interact with everyone is consistent with the way they are expected to train their children to interact with others, and that is critical because children typically interact with others in the way they've observed role models interacting with others.

Subjects will include the psychology of a child's development, the effect that the parents' behavior has on the child's development, and the procedure for training the child to follow the basic precept in all that the child does. Prospective parents will also be shown how to nurture and encourage their children so that all children realize full potential as a viable and productive member of their family and of the society to which the children and their family belong. The key is getting the parents to understand that their child is an individual and is entitled to the same respect and treatment they expect for themselves as individuals.

To ensure that all potential parents get this training, all parents will be required to obtain a permit before having a baby, and in order to get a permit, both potential parents will be required to take the classes mentioned previously and will have to be evaluated to determine whether they are capable of providing an emotionally stable environment in which to raise the child they wish to have. By requiring couples wishing to have a child to obtain a permit, population growth can be controlled and that will improve the chances that every child who is born will enjoy a full and rewarding life.

In order to ensure that everyone obtains a permit before having a child, the government will offer compelling incentives. Those who obtain a permit to have a baby qualify to receive free education, free childcare, free aptitude evaluation, and free health care for the baby both before and after the baby is born. On the other hand, if a couple does not get a permit before having a baby, the baby will be removed from the couple's care at birth and given to a couple that has obtained a permit to have a baby, but has not been able to produce one.

In addition, birth records will be checked to determine if either of the biological parents involved has given birth to another baby without first obtaining a permit. If not, both will be warned that failure to obtain a permit before having another baby will result in sterilization of the repeat offender. If either or both have already been warned, they will be sterilized.

The government will pay for the replacement of each individual who is old enough to sexually reproduce. Therefore a couple is entitled to have two children. However, there will always be individuals who do not want or are unable to have children, and there will be those who reach sexual maturity and die before they can reproduce. So, if a couple who already has two children wants more, the couple will be allowed to do so if the two satisfy all the requirements for obtaining a permit and there is a worldwide deficit in the number of children being produced by their generation.

To ensure that people who don't or can't have children are able to genetically contribute to improving humanity's ability to evolve as the Earth's living environment evolves, it is essential that a system be implemented that ensures that every individual's DNA is preserved. This should be done so that if later analysis determines that a person's bodily characteristics have enabled that person to function more effectively in environmental conditions that adversely affect contemporaries who have been exposed to the same conditions, the DNA could be analyzed to try to isolate the genetic coding that produced the beneficial characteristic. That way, once the coding has been identified, prenatal procedures can be used to introduce that coding into all subsequent embryos in order to accelerate the natural selection process. Such a procedure will make it more likely that all people whose bodies contain genetic material that produces an improvement in human physical or mental functionality will be able to contribute that improvement whether they produce children of their own or not.

CHAPTER 24

Teach All Children That Everyone's Well-being Is Equally Important

If you are raising a young child or you are now a grandparent of a young child, you know that a newborn's total focus is on its own needs, comfort, and happiness. That self-absorption is essential to the newborn's survival and development into a healthy, productive individual. However, as each baby matures, it must be taught that its needs are no more important than the needs of the other members of its immediate family. It must also be taught that the needs of every other human being on Earth are just as important as its own.

Today, there is no consistency in the way infant human beings are taught how to behave as adults. That's because child raising techniques are handed down from one generation to the next and few question their effectiveness. Furthermore, as mentioned previously, since all young children are impressionable, poor nurturing usually insures that the children will become poor nurturers. Since every human infant comes into this world with no preconceived opinions, the parents have an incumbent responsibility to teach their child that all life has a purpose and that the child must respect that premise and act accordingly. On the other hand, it is incumbent on parents to teach their children caution when interacting with any form of living thing with which they are not familiar. However, in order for these measures to be effective, prospective parents must make the conscious decision to avoid all behavior that demonstrates selfishness, prejudice, superstition, and bigotry before they produce a child. Then, when the child is born, they must have already started treating all life forms the way they want their children to treat all life forms that they may encounter during their lifetime. This is essential because a parent's most effective means of teaching a child desirable behavior is by demonstrating it in the process of dealing with the vicissitudes of daily living.

Obviously, eliminating selfishness, prejudice, superstition, and bigotry requires overcoming a predilection for adhering to the same behavioral attitudes and habits espoused or demonstrated by previous generations, but that is very difficult to accomplish unless a concerted effort is made, through education, to show people how alternatives generate more constructive results for future generations. The problem is motivation. Why should people change the way they have always done things? The solution is to teach all children on Earth that every other human being on Earth is just as important to the species as they are, and that humanity will never succeed in making Earth an enjoyable place to live for everyone until each of us learns to treat others the way we want to be treated. They must also be taught to have the same concern for how the Earth and all life on Earth is treated as they have for the way they and their most valued loved ones and acquaintances are treated.

Children learn from observing how others react to the words and actions of those who command positions of importance in the child's mind. Obviously, the people most influential on a young child are the child's parents and siblings followed closely by influential members of a child's extended family. Characters in the books and cartoons that the child is exposed to can also be a powerful influence. Since all children develop their character from what they perceive to be acceptable and unacceptable behavior by the people the child observes in real-life situations or from situations portrayed in plays, movies, story books, and television, it's essential that children's external influences be restricted to those that demonstrate the kind of behavior that the children are expected to emulate so they develop the desired behavioral traits.

Probably the first thing that registers with children is whether their own actions and attempts at speaking cause pleasant or unpleasant reactions. Since human beings prefer pleasant reactions, a child learns quickly to discard behavior that results in an unpleasant reaction. But here is where it gets tricky for the parent. Children mimic behavior they've observed parents and siblings engaging in, especially when the observed behavior elicits pleasant reactions from others, but if the mimicked behavior brings an unpleasant reaction when the child does it, the child is likely to be confused. Therefore, a child's parents, siblings, teachers, and others who regularly interact with an impressionable child must be consistent in their behavior when the child is present. That means parents should take care to ensure that their own behavior sets the example they want their child to emulate. They must also be proactive in ensuring that the effect of everyone else's behavior in the presence of their child reinforces the behavior to which the child is expected to adhere.

Controlling how people behave in a child's presence is one thing. Controlling a child's exposure to undesirable media content requires even more effort. That's because parents must be constantly aware of whether the books, movies, TV programs, and plays that their children may be exposed to are portraying unacceptable behavior, and they must do everything they can to minimize their children's exposure to undesirable content conveyed in these media.

In summary, a child's parents are responsible for creating a learning environment in which all parties that interact with their child in any way, either directly or indirectly, model only acceptable behavior in the child's presence. Furthermore, they must learn to react consistently to a child's behavior in order to reinforce the child's perception of which kinds of behavior are acceptable and which behavior kinds of behavior are unacceptable. That way, everyone with whom the child interacts will project consistent expectations and will be consistent in modeling those expectations. This will ensure that the children in their care will be more likely to develop the kind of character they'll need to have in order to become accepted members of their own family as well as the community in which they live.

The toughest part of carrying out this plan of action is being able to spend the time it takes to accomplish the plan's objective. There are two options. The time-honored option is for one parent or both to commit to providing the desired learning environment by teaching the child at home and having the child accompany parents in all that they do. The less demanding option is to allow others to participate in this process, but this option requires exhausting due diligence and performance monitoring in order to ensure that everyone who interacts with their children during the process of educating and caring for them is doing their job properly.

Bottom line: raising children properly requires the parents' total commitment to ensuring their children's welfare while helping them become self-confident individuals who are able to utilize their skills and talents to sustain an adequate standard of living.

SECTION 2

Involve All Humans in Establishing a World Community Attitude

In order to establish a worldwide attitude of community, the majority of Earth's human population must be willing to get involved in making it happen, and it will require the same kind of resolve as has been exhibited in the civil rights movement that is ongoing in the United States. The first step in getting involved is for people to modify their lifestyles so that every aspect of their behavior reflects the practice of mutual empathy and adherence to the basic precept. In other words, involvement requires adopting a common deliberative process when deciding how to act on, or react to each situation that arises in the course of daily living. The idea is to establish a worldwide community of individuals who use the same deliberative process in deciding how to deal with or accomplish each task they believe is necessary to sustain an acceptable lifestyle and make their life as pleasant as possible.

People will have become involved when they conscientiously begin doing the things that eliminate problems for themselves, others, or for Earth's living environment. That's because they will have replaced their attitude of entitlement with an attitude of inclusiveness, and they will have learned to subordinate their ego-driven behavior to behavior that is considerate of others as well as all aspects of their living environment that their actions or activities may affect. Furthermore, the positive results obtained by these changes in behavior and attitude will set an example for others to emulate because it will influence them to reconsider how their behavior affects the various aspects of life on Earth.

Once enough people have become involved in this way, they can begin to create an organization of involved persons so that their efforts to get others involved and to get results will be more proactive. The following chapters discuss the steps that must be taken for these involved persons' organizations to coalesce into a worldwide network of organizations that are all striving to attain the desired result, namely, a worldwide community of human beings who are committed to making Earth as hospitable a place to live as possible and to counteracting all attitudes, activities, and behavior that inhibit that from happening.

CHAPTER 25

Create Involved Persons' Networks and Enroll Participants

The first step in bringing about a shift in the attitude people have regarding themselves, other human beings, and the rest of creation on Earth is to initiate a concerted effort to get people to commit to be more directly involved in creating a community attitude within the area where they live. This usually begins when one individual is willing to set an example that stimulates others to emulate that behavior or attitude. Eventually, if enough people buy in to its effectiveness, that initial effort will stimulate an even more influential movement that can bring about a shift in a community's attitude regarding which ways of doing things are acceptable and which are not.

Some may doubt that such a shift can actually happen, but human history is full of instances in which the will of the people ultimately forced significant changes to take place. Perhaps the most impressive example occurred in the early part of the twentieth century when a man named Mahatma Gandhi taught his followers how to use nonviolent civil disobedience to force Great Britain to abandon its colonial government in India and allow India to become a self-governing nation. Other instances that come to mind are England's King John being forced to accept the Magna Carta in 1215 to avoid rebellion by his barons; Thomas Paine's pamphlet *Common Sense* written in 1776, which called for America's independence from England; and the Gandhi-inspired civil disobedience by African Americans in the 1950s that influenced the U.S. Supreme Court to strike down laws requiring segregation of blacks from whites on buses in Montgomery,

Alabama. In the latter instance, that ruling initiated a shift in attitudes by whites who had previously supported rules that denied former slaves and their descendants equal access to public places and facilities. John F. Kennedy encouraged people to "Ask not what your country can do for you, ask what you can do for your country." That admonition succinctly places into perspective what being involved entails.

In order to develop an attitude of community among all Earth's human beings, the majority of Earth's human population must be willing to get involved to the same extent as those groups who were and are involved in the civil rights movement. This is because that kind of involvement is essential in establishing the kind of resolve that will be required to bring about the transition from the geopolitical circumstances that exist today to a worldwide community of human beings who willingly share Earth, its resources, and the produce of those resources equitably.

In most governmental organizations today, democracy's effectiveness is negated by special interest groups because these groups are able to use their resources to manipulate the democratic process for personal gain. They do this by using contributions from like-minded people to help get persons elected who will vote the way the special interest groups want them to. That way, they are able to get legislation passed that results in the best outcome for their special interests and to block legislation that doesn't. To establish a more equitable way of doing things, the system must be changed, and the only way to do that is to replace special interest politics with a system that ensures that those who are elected to represent humanity's collective best interests actually do so. Obviously, the only way such a change will happen is for enough people to decide that special interest politics is unacceptable and that changes must be made that eliminate the practice.

Before a person can become involved, that person needs to understand what that means. Therefore, individuals must learn how to integrate both mutual empathy and the basic precept into their lifestyle so that when they act on, or react to, the situations with which they are confronted in the course of living their lives, their behaviors will reflect the influence of both. When they do that they will have become involved because they will have begun to use a common deliberative process in deciding how they will accomplish all the tasks they believe necessary to not only sustain them and make their own lives as pleasant as possible, but also help others do likewise.

This kind of behavior encourages others to do likewise, and as more and more people emulate this kind of behavior, a worldwide community of like-minded individuals will materialize who have adopted the same approach to accomplishing their chosen lifestyle. In other words, regardless of the lifestyle they choose to pursue, people will have learned to avoid doing anything that threatens humanity's well-being, and they will have learned to do the kinds of things that are good for themselves as well as everyone and everything else that shares creation with them. In addition, people's attitudes of personal entitlement will have been replaced by attitudes of inclusion, and their ego-driven behavior will have been replaced by behavior considerate of others as well as all aspects of creation that their actions and activities affect. Furthermore, when people become involved, they will feel compelled to encourage everyone they encounter who doesn't appear to already be involved to replace their attitude of entitlement with an attitude of involvement. Likewise, in elections they'll support candidates whose demonstrated commitment to practicing the basic precept and mutual empathy indicates their willingness to help transform Earth into a worldwide community of human beings who all share a similar mind-set.

For most people, letting their actions and behavior model an exemplary lifestyle and encouraging others to do likewise is as involved as they wish to be. For some people, however, this level of commitment isn't enough. They'd like to be more proactive in coordinating their activities with the activities of others in order to be more effective in encouraging everyone to engage in behavior motivated by mutual empathy and guided by the basic precept.

For those involved persons wishing to be more proactive in coordinating their activities with the activities of others in their area as well in adjacent areas, they will need to establish a network of involved persons that enables involved persons living in close proximity to one another to coordinate their efforts to encourage use of the basic precept and mutual empathy and discourage violations of the basic precept and mutual empathy. The objective of these networks is to eliminate all harmful behavior that is threatening the well-being of some aspect of creation in their area and to establish a community in which all are encouraged to live productive lives that are compatible with all aspects of creation their behavior affects. In other words, the primary focus of all involved persons is to let their own behavior be a model for the kind of behavior they want everyone else to emulate, namely, letting mutual empathy and the basic precept influence every aspect of their behavior.

Initially, the number of involved persons living within an area will be insufficient to be effective and it is likely that those who are practicing mutual empathy and the basic precept will not be aware of others living in close proximity that are doing likewise. Therefore, it will be necessary to establish a means of communication that enables practitioners of the basic precept and mutual empathy to find and communicate with other practitioners who live nearby. It will also be necessary to develop a missionary operation that targets areas in which no practitioners are known to live. In other words, involved persons who live in other areas will have to take it upon themselves to organize efforts to assume that responsibility and begin the process of teaching the concepts to a targeted area's residents one person at a time until sufficient numbers of residents from the targeted area have reached the point at which they can take over the teaching task themselves.

In some areas, this kind of activity will require the initial involved persons to work clandestinely in order to accomplish their objective while avoiding confrontation with those who oppose this kind of effort because it adversely affects some advantage they enjoy from the status quo. In extreme instances where an area is dominated by people with special interests that are threatened by the desired shift in people's attitudes that this kind of movement will affect, relocation of those who are being taken advantage of may be the best alternative.

Obviously, relocation of people will require coordination within and between area networks, so internetwork communication will need to be implemented in order to facilitate the accomplishment of network endeavors. In other words, in order for involved persons' networking to be effective, every involved person must be able to maintain constant awareness of what is happening, not only in their part of the world, but in other parts of the world as well, particularly when what is happening violates the basic precept or the practice of mutual empathy and is negatively impacting some aspect of creation on Earth.

When the problem affects some aspect of creation within the area that includes their place of residence, involved persons can use personal interaction to coordinate their attempts to dissuade those causing the problem from continuing to engage in the problematic activity, particularly those activities that negatively impact other human beings living in their area or diminish some aspect of the Earth's ability to sustain the health and well-being of all aspects of creation within their area. When the problem is in a part of the world where involved persons have no direct influence, they must urge business leaders and government officials they know who do have influence to use that influence to persuade the local officials where the problem exists to take whatever corrective action is necessary to eliminate the human behavior or practices that are causing the problem. In other words, people who adhere to the basic precept and practice mutual empathy must coordinate their economic and political activities as well as their personal involvement in order to influence the way things are done everywhere on Earth so that everyone and everything on Earth is able to successfully sustain their existence while living in as pollution free an environment as possible.

Keeping all involved persons informed will require the implementation of inter network and intra network communication. Given the status of communications technology, perhaps the best way to keep everyone informed within a network is to use pocket-sized, computerized devices that enable people to communicate with one another using some form of social networking software. In other words, the technology already exists that enables individuals to communicate verbally or via text messages with other individuals or with multiple individuals simultaneously. This will enable members of an involved persons' network to instantaneously alert all other members of their network when any of them becomes aware of an activity taking place in their area that is enhancing or adversely affecting some aspect of life in the area where they live.

The content of these kinds of messages would describe the activity that has been observed and identify the individuals, government officials, and businessmen involved. Having this kind of information will enable involved persons to make informed decisions about products they will buy and use, companies they will invest in, businesses they will patronize or boycott, government officials they will support or oppose, and individuals they will associate with or avoid.

The same kind of communication system can be used for keeping all area networks informed about what is going on in all other networks. This is particularly useful when tracking the activities of people or organizations whose operations transcend the boundaries of one area's network. In those instances, internetwork communication is essential in order to coordinate all efforts made by involved persons to address a given situation that requires their attention.

For example, if it has been verified that a particular company is violating the basic precept in its treatment of its employees, the involved persons within the applicable area networks can be encouraged to boycott that company's products or services and they, in turn, can initiate a campaign to persuade noninvolved friends and neighbors to do the same. In other words, involved persons can use purchasing power to encourage companies to use mutual empathy in their dealings with others and to adhere to the basic precept in all aspects of their business. They can also use their vote to elect officials who are committed to enacting rules and regulations that are consistent with the practice of mutual empathy and an adherence to the basic precept.

Once involved persons' networks are able to communicate amongst themselves, they will become very effective in influencing everyone to be more diligent in practicing mutual empathy and adhering to the basic precept. That's because they will have the ability to identify people who are not practicing mutual empathy or adhering to the basic precept and coordinate efforts to influence them to change or risk becoming isolated to the point that they are no longer relevant. This should ultimately result in everyone choosing to practice mutual empathy and adhere to the basic precept to avoid becoming outcasts. When that happens, a world community attitude will have been established.

In order for involved persons' networks to be optimally effective in these activities, every involved person must strive to remain constantly vigilant for any occurrence of behavior in their area that violates the basic precept and negatively impacts human rights or some other aspect of life in their community. They must also be relentless in keeping themselves informed about what is being done to alleviate those situations. That way, when they discover a situation that adversely affects living conditions within the area that includes their place of residence, they can use their purchasing power, their voting power, and any other means of persuasion available to them to dissuade the persons or businesses involved from continuing to engage in the problem-causing activity.

The situations that involved persons should be most concerned about are ones that involve any activity that directly impacts other human beings or diminishes some aspect of Earth's ability to sustain the health and well-being of some aspect of creation. When the area in which they live is being affected, they must become personally involved in persuading those responsible for causing the problem to stop engaging in the activities that are causing the problem. When the problem causing activity is in another part of the world, they must lobby business leaders and government officials who have influence in the affected area to use that influence to persuade the local officials where the problem exists to take whatever corrective action is most likely to eliminate the behavior and practices causing the problem.

Ultimately, these kinds of activities should be effective in persuading all people to adopt the basic precept and use mutual empathy as guidelines for how they treat others, and when that happens, the groundwork will have been laid for the establishment of peace on Earth.

CHAPTER 26

Additional Thoughts Related to the Universal Use of the Basic Precept and Mutual Empathy

Most nations in the world today are reluctant to relinquish their sovereignty to the extent necessary to enable the sharing of Earth's resources equitably. That's because most nations in the world are controlled by a privileged minority who use their influence to ensure that the allocation of their nation's resources benefits them disproportionately. As a result, the less privileged in those nations are prevented from obtaining the wherewithal needed to sustain an adequate lifestyle, and they are stymied in their efforts to improve their circumstances. Therefore, it is the responsibility of people living elsewhere who are practitioners of mutual empathy and the basic precept to try to provide in-place assistance to those in need unless the political circumstances within the nation where those in need live make that option impossible.

If in-place assistance is not permitted by those in power where people are in need, alternative efforts to alleviate the situation must be undertaken. The first alternative is to raise public awareness of the situation. This can be accomplished by initiating campaigns to influence the appropriate politicians to get involved and by publicizing the situation to as wide an audience as possible. If this alternative fails to get results or the actions taken are insufficient, then the second alternative is to undertake clandestine operations by involved private citizens to alleviate the deprivation, first by providing in-place assistance if that is possible then by providing relocation assistance if in-place assistance is not possible. In the latter instance, the objective is to help those in need relocate from the nation that is allowing deprivation or other mistreatment to take place to a nation that offers acceptable living conditions and will permit them to begin new lives there.

The relocation option would require that there be involved persons already in the country of origin who are willing to facilitate these kinds of relocations. These involved persons may be natural born citizens in the country of origin or they may be involved persons from other countries who have immigrated to the country of origin for the express purpose of initiating clandestine operations to help mistreated persons who live in the country of origin. There must also be involved persons living in the receiving nation who are willing to take in the persons being relocated there and help them get through immigration, find lodging, and obtain work so that they can quickly become productive citizens who are accepted within their new community.

Economic and political pressure will eventually influence nations that tolerate violations of mutual empathy and the basic precept to change their ways, but in the meantime something must be done to help those who are suffering abuse or deprivation because of the way the country in which they live is being governed. There are still places in the world where those in control are aware of the fact that at least some of their people are not able to sustain themselves with what they are able to gather or produce on their own, but they either can't or choose not to alleviate the situation. Perhaps doing nothing better serves their purposes or perhaps they simply do not have the wherewithal to respond. Either way, the network of involved persons must do what it can to help satisfy the needs of those who are suffering as a result.

When the nation in which a need exists welcomes outside assistance, the involved persons' network nearest the nation in need can negotiate with government officials to determine the kinds of assistance needed then coordinate the involved persons' response in providing that assistance. When people in control of a nation in which a problem exists are either condoning the problem-causing behavior or are complicit in the behavior causing the problem, involved people must use their networks to provide the needed assistance clandestinely while doing what they can to publicize the situation to raise public awareness and influence public opinion.

When any aspect of creation on Earth is endangered by natural events or by mistreatment, and the place where the problem exists is controlled by people who are either causing the problem or are allowing the problem to exist for self-serving reasons, the network of involved persons nearest the nation where the problem exists will organize teams of involved persons from their area who are willing to operate clandestinely to provide relief for the aspect of creation being abused. The objective is to provide assistance to those who need it without those in power being aware of what is going on or being able to benefit in any way from the assistance being provided.

The kinds of assistance provided will depend on the circumstances and conditions that must be dealt with. Typically, the team of involved persons who live nearest those who need assistance will be the ones who provide it. If the assistance requires provisions that that team does not have and cannot acquire without drawing attention to its efforts, word will be passed to other areas where involved persons operate so the required provisions can be acquired elsewhere and then passed from involved person to involved person until the provisions reach the team that made the request. This type of operation requires involved persons in every country on Earth to make the commitment to help their neighbors and others who are being mistreated or abused either by handling the problem themselves or by joining with other, like-minded individuals who are willing to do whatever needs to be done to alleviate the problem.

When in-place assistance is not feasible, the involved persons who are providing assistance will help relocate those being deprived of acceptable living conditions to a safe haven where they can be accommodated until conditions in their home country improve and they can return home, or until they can be prepared for a new life elsewhere and arrangements can be made to relocate them there. The objective is to help innocent bystanders get out of harm's way when they are caught in a situation that threatens their safety and well-being, and those responsible for causing the situation are impervious to the effect their actions are having on these innocent bystanders.

People taking action to alleviate mistreatment by others is not a new concept. The involved persons' attempts to help people who are suffering as the result of being in the wrong place at the wrong time would be similar to the underground railroad that operated in the United States in the years prior to the beginning of the Civil War in 1860. Back then, it was private citizens helping freed slaves relocate from southern states where they were being discriminated against to northern states where they were allowed to live as free persons. Today, it would involve private citizens facilitating the movement of people from and supplies to countries where living conditions are below the minimum acceptable standard and lives are being endangered by self-serving human behavior.

To be sure, there are already plenty of organizations whose mission is to assist people in need, but all these organizations operate under the auspices of the governmental authority whose jurisdiction includes the places where their assistance is provided. Consequently, they have limited freedom to relocate persons living in other countries who are deemed to live in intolerable situations. To address this, an independent organization is required that is willing to operate without the permission of the local authorities to get the desired results.

As with the aforementioned underground railroad operation, the originating places for relocation efforts would be the homes of involved persons who live in the country of origin and are willing to provide food, rest, and protection while making arrangements to help people who wish to leave the country in which they have been living. Then, these people would be assisted in moving to and from a succession of safe houses along the way until they reach a facility operated by involved persons that is located in the nearest neighboring country that condones the involved persons' activities.

Some might question the effectiveness of this kind of operation, but not only did it work in America before and during the Civil War, it also worked in France during the German occupation at the beginning of World War II. In the latter instance, the French underground helped allied airmen and others, who were trapped in France, get out of areas controlled by the Germans and into areas controlled by the allied forces. In both instances, the networks were successful because they were made up of persons who knew each other, had a common goal, and were determined to overcome seemingly insurmountable odds.

Present day involved persons' clandestine operations would be no different. It simply takes concerned people in every part of the world deciding to act on their own and in concert with like-minded individuals to develop an organization that facilitates the movement of supplies into and, if necessary, people out of countries where they are being deprived of the opportunity to live satisfactorily.

In order to prevent agents of the privileged minority from infiltrating the underground network so they can sabotage it, no one would be allowed to become involved in clandestine operations without first becoming part of an involved persons' network. Since persons wishing to join an involved persons' network have to be corroborated as practicing mutual empathy and living by the basic precept, if they are found to be eligible for membership in the involved persons' network, then they are also eligible to become active in clandestine operations if they choose to do so.

When the need for clandestine help is in an area where clandestine operations have no representatives, a member of the involved persons' network closest to the area where help is needed will investigate to determine if the need warrants clandestine assistance. If so, the investigating member will take up residence in the target area and begin to determine whether there are people living in the area that appear to adhere to the basic precept and practice mutual empathy. The objective is to identify and approach people living in the area who might be willing to become involved and join the involved persons' network once they understand that its mission is to assist people living in their area who are being deprived of the wherewithal to live their lives at or above the minimum acceptable level of existence.

As things are now, if people live in a country where they are not able to get enough to sustain themselves in a viable existence, they are at the mercy of the country's government, and there are a lot of governments that are not willing or are not able to provide the necessary assistance. If a country is not able to provide the necessary assistance and it is willing to allow outside agencies in, there are international agencies that can provide the assistance needed. Unfortunately, there are countries in which those in control do not want outsiders to help directly. Instead, they prefer to receive contributions and then distribute the contributions themselves. That way, they are able to control which people benefit most from the assistance provided. When this kind of system is utilized, some with needs are short changed because those responsible for providing assistance misappropriate that assistance in order to enrich themselves and their friends.

People who are intentionally deprived by their government or by their government's representatives have few options if they want a better life. In fact, they only have one. If they want the opportunity to have a more fulfilling existence, they must leave their own country and enter a country where they can find work that allows them to support themselves as well as family members left behind. However, most countries to which people want to immigrate have immigration quotas, so people who are denied legal entry often choose to enter these countries illegally. Consequently, they have to deal constantly with the possibility that they will be caught and forced to return to their country of origin. But even if they don't get caught, entering another country illegally can be risky, because the countries that illegal immigrants are trying to enter are usually countries that are trying to prevent them from doing so. Therefore, illegal immigrants are forced to take risks that endanger their well-being.

The involved persons' network provides an alternative that is less stress-ful for the illegal immigrant and less costly for those countries to which illegal immigrants want to go. The network enables people who want a better life to obtain it while avoiding the pitfalls of illegal immigration. This is accomplished by smuggling needed assistance in to those who are not able to support them-selves due to oppressive conditions in the country where they reside.

In these circumstances, the involved persons' network will coordinate their efforts to not only help those in need, but also to address the causes of the prob-lem the immigrants are trying avoid. This is particularly true when the problem involves the deprivation of human beings' ability to live a healthy, productive life in a living environment that enables them to do that.

These kinds of activities, often undertaken clandestinely, are intended to influence those whose policies and practices are depriving targeted groups within their countries of adequate living conditions and sustenance. This is accomplished in several ways. One way is to help immigrants living in other countries send supplies to left-behind family members in their homeland. This will enable those still in the homeland to avoid having to buy the things they need to sustain themselves in the place where they live. In other words, immi-grants can buy the needed goods in the country to which they have immigrated and let the involved persons' clandestine operations network deliver the goods as well as money to left-behind family members in the country of origin. As a result, the merchants and government officials in the targeted country who are responsible for, or support such deprivation will be denied benefits they might have otherwise received. This kind of reverse deprivation will help moti-vate those with influence to initiate reforms that eliminate the practices that are causing this kind of deprivation to occur.

Funding for these types of activities will be derived from contributions by the immigrants themselves as well as from donations made by members of the involved persons' network and from donations made by people who want to be involved, but do not want to actively participate in network activities.

SECTION 3
Considerations for How to Extend Humanity's Time on Earth

The following chapters offer considerations regarding what humanity must do to extend the length of time that Earth will be able to sustain people at an acceptable level of existence. Obviously, we humans must learn to conserve the natural resources that are essential to our being able to continue residing on Earth. One step is to reduce the need to produce new products. We must also learn to live in ways that are more compatible with Earth's ability to renew itself.

CHAPTER 27

Reduce Demand for New Durable Goods by Introducing Exchange Programs

Since natural resources are consumed when any kind of implement is made or clothing is created or shelter is constructed, unless a resource is used up during its initial use (as is the case with food, water, and air) it is essential that whatever is made from natural resources be created and maintained in a way that enables that product to remain functional indefinitely unless further use is impracticable. When use of a durable product is no longer possible, remaining resources must be reclaimed and put to some other use.

In order to accommodate people's need for variety and different sizes in clothing as their bodies grow and shrink with age or changes in lifestyle, a universal exchange program needs to be created that enables people to obtain the items they need for the short period of time they're needed then return them so the same clothing can be used by others in the same way. This will reduce the need to produce new items unless the inventory of existing goods is no longer sufficient to satisfy the demand for replacements as older items wear out to the point that refurbishing is no longer feasible.

When people bring an item in for exchange, they will be charged for the wear the item incurred during the time it was in their possession and they'll pay for the difference in the price of the item they are returning and the item they are obtaining. For example, if someone returns a toy that was used by a two-year-old and wants to exchange it for a toy that will be used by a three- or four-year-old, that person will have to pay a charge for restoring the turned-in toy to like-new condition and they'll have to pay the difference between the price of the restored old toy and the price of the desired replacement. If the toy being turned in is so badly damaged it cannot be restored to working condition, the person turning in the toy will be charged the price of a replacement and placed on probation in which case, any further incidents of excessive abuse will result in suspension of that person's ability to acquire similar products.

Obviously, this policy would also apply to all other kinds of durable products including automobiles, dwellings, appliances, household utensils, automated tools, manually operated tools, conveyance devices, furniture, and all other products that require proper maintenance to ensure functionality for an indefinite period of time. Therefore, a person who wishes to acquire a new durable product must be required to turn in the item being replaced. For example, when clothing is no longer usable because it has been outgrown or has become dated, the owner must turn it in when acquiring a replacement and pay for any deferred maintenance that needs to be corrected to restore the garment to refurbished condition. On the other hand, if a garment is so worn that refurbishing it is not an option, it must still be turned in so it can be made into cleaning rags or be shredded and used as filler for padding or as insulation.

The same requirements would apply for other types of durable products, because, under no circumstances should any durable product simply be discarded as trash. If it breaks, the owner should have it repaired and continue using it until it wears out, then the owner should turn it in so reusable materials can be recycled and put to other uses. If the product is durable but not reusable after its initial use, for example, a food container, people should turn the container in when acquiring a replacement product so the container can be recycled and made into something else.

Human beings must become more diligent in acquiring only enough durable products to sustain an adequate standard of living and they must become more proactive in prolonging the useful life of every durable product they acquire in order to reduce the consumption of nonrenewable natural resources that will be required to produce a replacement. Such diligence will also reduce the amount of fuel consumed during the process of harvesting natural resources, transporting them to where they are converted into end products and then transporting those end products to distributors and consumer outlets. Furthermore, reducing fuel consumption also reduces the volume of hazardous residues that are produced by fuel combustion, which in turn, reduces the amount of nonrenewable resources that are consumed in the process of capturing and eliminating these residues, and it reduces the expense, time, and effort needed to counteract the effect these polluting residues have on the health and well-being of Earth's living creatures and on the effectiveness of Earth's life support systems.

Of course, the exchange concept is a drastic departure from the modern consumer mind-set, which is to use acquisitions to establish or maintain a desirable persona. If people can afford to do it, they buy new things whenever fashions change or design improvements are introduced and the replaced products are set aside to collect dust, donated to a charity, or thrown away. However, the exchange program offers a fourth alternative. People can take no longer wanted or needed items to an exchange and the exchange will issue them a receipt that entitles the holder to obtain similar items that have been turned in by someone else.

The exchange will only stock items that are in good condition, therefore it will refurbish turned-in items and charge the next owner a fee that covers the expenses it incurred while restoring the item to good condition. When an item is turned in and no item is available for exchange, the exchange will keep a log of items it has received according to size, type, etc. That way, every time a new item is received, it can notify people who have previously turned in a similar item and are still holding a receipt. The person holding the receipt with the oldest date in the log will be contacted first and given the opportunity to decide whether they want to exchange his or her receipt for the newly received item. If the person decides not to, then each succeeding person in the log will be contacted until an exchange is made. Alternatively, a person holding a receipt may be allowed to use his or her receipt and receive a credit against the purchase of some other item being offered by the exchange.

This kind of system will enable people to accumulate the durable products they need to sustain an adequate lifestyle and to maintain variety by purchasing refurbished products they need, but don't own and by trading in products they own, but can no longer use or are tired of using. This allows them to replace unwanted items with refurbished replacements that someone else has returned or traded in previously. This system will enable people to enjoy variety without having to purchase new products whose production depletes limited natural resources.

Of course, people would have to learn to be satisfied with acquiring refurbished replacements instead of acquiring new products, and that might be difficult for those who are trying to establish or maintain a desirable persona by acquiring new things whenever fashions and designs change. On the other hand, if they've eliminated their attitude of entitlement and have learned to engage in mutual empathy, they'll be willing to make these necessary attitudinal changes because they'll know that it's in everyone's best interest to do so.

In order to make the exchange program more effective, manufacturers of durable products such as clothing, appliances, vehicles, dwellings, and implements must be required to create the most long lasting products possible and they must be required to construct them modularly so that they can be upgraded without having to replace the entire product. Manufacturers should also be required to avoid marketing practices that tempt consumers to trade in serviceable products for replacements that perform the same function, but have a more appealing appearance.

Consumers, on the other hand, must be required to use the things they buy in the most cost effective way possible and to maintain those things so they last as long as possible. Furthermore, monitoring must be implemented to ensure that they do, so that if they don't, they'll be prevented from acquiring replacements for items that they have abused.

In summary, manufacturers and consumers alike must become more resolute in their efforts to conserve natural resources by eliminating the need to replace the whole product in order to improve a product's energy efficiency, functionality, and durability. Instead they must embrace a different paradigm, which is to continuously upgrade existing products using replaceable parts and components. Of course, occasional cosmetic changes such as fresh paint and swapping out interiors should be allowed so owners can avoid becoming bored with expensive products like houses and automobiles before their usefulness ends.

CHAPTER 28
Learn How to Live Green Effectively

Each of us needs to think seriously about how our behavior impacts Earth's natural resources and Earth's ability to support life. To start, consider the obvious:

> Every moment of our lives, every action we take depletes natural resources that may or may not be replaceable.

Each time each human being takes in a breath of air, he or she uses up a little of the oxygen in the Earth's atmosphere. That means Earth's seven billion people are taking oxygen out of the air every couple of seconds and replacing it with carbon dioxide and water vapor. Furthermore, all of Earth's other oxygen-breathing organisms are doing the same thing. So why doesn't Earth's atmosphere run out of oxygen, and why doesn't the carbon dioxide and water vapor that Earth's oxygen-breathing creatures exhale accumulate in the atmosphere where it contributes to global warming?

You probably know it's because Earth's green plants as well as certain kinds of bacteria and oceanic organisms are constantly creating oxygen as a byproduct of the complicated chemical process known as photosynthesis that these organisms use to produce the food they need to sustain themselves. It gets better. Guess what one of the raw materials is that photosynthesis requires? Carbon dioxide! In other words, organisms that use photosynthesis to manufacture their food take carbon dioxide out of the air and put oxygen back. Is that symbiosis or what?

Therefore, as long as there are sufficient organisms existing on Earth that use the carbon dioxide that air-breathing organisms produce to create the oxygen that air-breathing organisms require, all is well. Unfortunately, human beings are inventive sorts, and we're constantly creating ways to make life easier and more enjoyable. In fact, almost every human endeavor these days involves activities that result in oxygen being taken out of the atmosphere and being replaced with carbon dioxide or other gases. Plus, as living has become easier, the human population has exploded. As a result, more and more land is being cleared of its carbon dioxide-removing, oxygen-producing green plants in order to accommodate the needs of all these people. Furthermore, the residue from all these pollution-producing activities is also polluting Earth's water and is reducing its effectiveness as a living environment for aquatic organisms that use photosynthesis to produce oxygen.

Water pollution also affects water-based organisms that sequestor carbon dioxide absorbed from the atmosphere by using it to create their shells, because when the water in which these organisms live becomes too toxic from absorbing airborne pollutants, the organisms die, thereby reducing the capability to sequester some carbon dioxide indefinitely.

Why should this be of concern? Ever heard of the greenhouse effect? Well you're probably familiar with the all-glass buildings people use to grow plants that require climate control. These buildings let sunlight heat their interiors and regulate the heat allowed to escape in order to maintain ideal growing conditions. Earth's atmosphere functions much like a greenhouse. It lets the sunlight through to warm the air near the Earth's surface and restricts the warm air from dissipating back into space, but unlike a plant greenhouse, Earth's atmosphere is not easily regulated.

When carbon dioxide and certain other gases are produced at the Earth's surface, they enter the atmosphere where they remain and function like the glass in a greenhouse, but unlike a greenhouse that enables the grower to regulate the heat inside, there is no way to eliminate the heat being created at the Earth's surface. Fortunately, these gases eventually dissipate, but the rate of dissipation is presently less than the rate at which additional gases are being created at the Earth's surface. Consequently, the volume of these gases in the atmosphere is increasing, and the resulting effect is like adding more blankets to your bed to keep warm. The difference is, when you get uncomfortable in bed, you can add or remove blankets to achieve a more comfortable sleeping arrangement. On the other hand, the only way to prevent Earth's surface temperatures from rising beyond tolerable levels is to keep the volume of heat-trapping gases being produced at Earth's surface from exceeding the rate at which greenhouse gases already in the atmosphere are dissipating. That's not easy to do.

So, what can each of us do to help attain the required balance? If you read a newspaper, listen to talk radio, or watch the news and infomercials on TV, you're being constantly bombarded with expert opinions, but the bottom line is this:

Until each of us becomes constantly aware of how every action we take affects Earth's ability to function effectively, and until each of us commits to moderate all behavior and activities that adversely affect Earth's ability to function effectively, the survival of our species is not assured.

CHAPTER 29

Develop Ways to Convert
Trash to Energy

Let's talk about biodegradable garbage. Where do you think your garbage goes after the waste disposal people pick it up and haul it off? Most of it is dumped into landfills where it decomposes in a limited oxygen environment that causes ground water pollution and creates methane gas. Methane gas has the same energy-producing component as natural gas, but it also becomes a very effective greenhouse gas when it escapes into the atmosphere. Therefore, biodegradable garbage must be disposed of in a way that prevents ground water pollution and enables reclamation of all reusable materials including the methane gas produced by the way we dispose of biodegradable garbage.

It turns out that some 425 dumps in the United States have been rigged to capture methane gas and use it to produce electricity. According to John Donnelly of the *Boston Globe*, almost eight hundred thousand homes in the United States get their electricity from power plants that use garbage dump methane gas to generate that electricity. One million, two hundred thousand residences are being heated using garbage dump methane gas.

In order for a garbage dump to produce cost-effective amounts of methane, it must be large, it must have been in use long enough for its contents to have sufficiently decayed and it must be covered in a way that restricts exposure to oxygen from the atmosphere and prevents the methane gas from seeping out of the dump and into the atmosphere. In other words, the most effective methane-producing dumps are large landfills that have been filled up and covered over with clay-based soil for an extended period of time.

In the United States, the Environmental Protection Agency (EPA) regulates all landfills to control release of greenhouse gas into the atmosphere, but it does not appear that any federal government agency has been given the responsibility of replacing small municipal dumps with a national network of large landfills that have been rigged to capture the methane gas such dumps will eventually produce and transport it via pipelines to an integrated network of processing plants where it can be converted to a useable energy source. This is significant because the process can be used to supplement the sources of energy presently being derived from dwindling underground deposits of oil, natural gas, and coal.

There are already municipalities in United States that have done these dump modifications and have begun collecting the gas theses dumps produce. Furthermore, there are plenty of other places in the world where this technique is already being used. Plants are reported to be operational in Belarus, Ukraine, Poland, Turkey, Azerbaijan, Slovenia, Latvia, Hungary, and Croatia. Additional sites are under construction in Croatia, Hungary, and Poland; are in the design stage in Ukraine; and are in the planning stage in Ukraine, Bulgaria, Slovenia, Azerbaijan, Hungary, and Belarus. Initial sites are in the planning stage in Romania, Serbia, and Lithuania. Still, the majority of nations on Earth have not yet undertaken this systematic disposal of their biodegradable waste. So in order to help solve humanity's need for renewable sources of energy and its need to reduce the volume of greenhouse gases being released into the atmosphere, it is essential that all biodegradable garbage be disposed of in this manner.

In order to make this happen, a worldwide oversight organization needs to be created and given the following responsibilities:

- Establish guidelines for the proper disposition of biodegradable waste so ground and water pollution is minimized and recovery of reusable resources is maximized;
- Establish a network of regional landfills that enable the capture of sequestered gas, water, and other materials that can be put to uses that reduce depletion of naturally occurring resources;
- Ensure that adequate infrastructure is developed to utilize reclaimed resources;
- Establish penalties for noncompliance and create an enforcement agency responsible for inspections and for issuing of citations to violators.

Such an oversight organization could also be made responsible for developing similar programs for manufacturing and product use to ensure that these activities do not produce residues harmful to the environment or deplete non-renewable natural resources excessively.

The framework for such an organization already exists in the United Nations Environment Programme (UNEP). UNEP has done an excellent job of defining the problems, identifying the pollutants, and analyzing the effect on the environment and Earth's fauna and flora. However, it doesn't appear that this agency has any authority to make rules and enforce them. Instead, it relies on member nations to interpret the information UNEP provides and develop its own rules and regulations for controlling the activities and behavior creating the problems. As a result, there is no worldwide consistency in the law pertaining to these issues or to the enforcement of those laws.

Therefore, the nations of the world must acquiesce to the UNEP by allowing it to define what constitutes polluting activity or behavior and by implementing universally consistent rules, regulations, and enforcement procedures that ensure all people are on the same page with regard to making Earth a better, safer, more enjoyable place to live. Furthermore, UNEP must be given policing authority that allows it to ensure that its rules and regulations are being consistently adhered to by all nations. Until that happens, the status quo will prevail and Earth's human inhabitants will continue to be at an impasse regarding how to bring about the changes required to prolong the time during which Earth will be inhabitable.

SECTION 4

Facilitating Humanity's Coalescence into a Worldwide Community

The following is a catalog of the various services that would need to be made available to all individuals regardless of where on Earth they live. The order in which these services are discussed does not necessarily imply the order in which each should be implemented. Rather, the discussion is intended to introduce the steps that must be taken if humanity is ever going to coalesce into a worldwide community. The ensuing chapters will expand on what each step entails.

ESTABLISH A WORLD GOVERNING STRUCTURE

Obviously, the first step in providing consistent worldwide services is to establish an organization with the authority to implement such services. The most expedient way to do that is to modify the United Nations charter to give it overriding authority for ensuring that all Earth's citizens have equal rights and are allowed to share in Earth's resources on an equal basis. In other words, the United Nations should be given the authority to establish guidelines for acceptable behavior all over the world and the means for ensuring that all sovereign nations honor those guidelines in dealings with their own citizens and with other sovereign nations and the citizens of other sovereign nations. In addition, the United Nations should assume control of all Earth's land and its resources and be responsible for overseeing the use of that land and those resources in the way that benefits all Earth's inhabitants equitably. Finally, the United Nations should be responsible for establishing the following:

A WORLDWIDE MEANS FOR MAINTAINING LAW AND ORDER

An agency within the United Nations' governing structure will be charged with developing, implementing, and enforcing a set of behavioral guidelines that all persons worldwide will be required to follow in their interactions with other human beings and with Earth and its natural resources.

A WORLDWIDE EDUCATION SYSTEM

An agency within the United Nations governing structure would be responsible for developing all educational programs and for ensuring that these programs are taught consistently everywhere on Earth. The agency would also be responsible for implementing a worldwide system that prepares persons of all ages to handle every aspect of life that they are likely to face during their lifetimes.

WORLDWIDE CONTROL OVER USE OF NATURAL RESOURCES

An agency within the United Nations governing structure would own all Earth's land and its natural resources, and that group would control use of Earth's land and its resources in order to ensure that all human beings on Earth have adequate housing and are able to obtain the wherewithal to sustain themselves in an acceptable standard of living.

WORLDWIDE MANAGEMENT OF ECONOMIC ACTIVITY

An agency within the United Nations governing structure would be responsible for implementing a universal monetary system, tracking human population growth, and managing the economic infrastructure required to meet the needs of Earth's human population.

WORLDWIDE HEALTH MAINTENANCE

An agency within the United Nations structure would be responsible for implementing a universal health care system in charge of ensuring the health and well-being of all Earth's human beings.

CHAPTER 30

Establish a Worldwide Governing Structure

A world governing structure must be established to assume the responsibility of creating the infrastructure within which the world's present political entities will operate. This infrastructure comprises a congress divided into two chambers, a chief operating officer and operational departments responsible for managing government affairs. The world's citizens will elect representatives to both chambers of congress, and the congress will define the functions of government as well as choose and oversee the persons who will carry out the functions of government including the government's chief operating officer. Congress will also establish the laws that define acceptable behavior and modify or clarify them as the need arises.

One chamber of congress will be made up of a representative from every identifiable ethnic group in existence when the world community begins operating. Each ethnic group's representative will be elected by all persons who are registered as a member of that ethnic group. The other chamber of congress will be made up of precinct representatives who have been elected by all the people living within the precinct that the candidate wishes to represent. Each precinct will be delineated so that it contains approximately the same number of residents as all other precincts. Every ten years, precinct boundaries will be adjusted and new precincts added or subtracted to accommodate changes in the number of citizens and the distribution of those citizens around the world.

Ethnicity will be used to define the electorate for one chamber of congress because in the beginning, giving all ethnic groups equal standing will be essential in gaining everyone's support. Everyone will want to make sure his or her ethnic group has as much influence as those whose group has enjoyed favored status in the past. Of course, these petty jealousies and prejudices will eventually go away as everyone learns to use his or her mutual empathy and the basic precept, and when that happens, the focus of the representatives for each ethnic group will be on preserving its ethnic heritage and addressing any problems that may be endemic to its ethnicity.

Each person's vote will be cast and counted using that person's implanted microcomputer. Details about how each person's implanted microcomputer works are discussed in chapter 35.

When the voter enters the voting booth, the booth's computer will be able to interact with the voter's implanted microcomputer via wireless interface to determine in which precinct the voter is eligible to vote. Afterward, the voting booth's communications screen will present the candidates for the voter's precinct representative and the candidates for the voter's ethnic representative. The voter will choose the candidates he or she wants to vote for and then indicate to the booth computer that he or she is ready for his or her vote to be tallied. The voting computer will then tally the person's votes, and at the end of the day, it will transmit its vote totals to a central computer that tallies vote totals for each position being contested.

The governing infrastructure will be organized into operational departments, each with a director who is picked by and is accountable to the governing structure's chief operating officer. The directors are nominated by the chief operating officer and approved by the congress. Managers within each departmental group are selected by their department director, but must be approved by an independent agency of the basic precept control group.

The operational agencies within the governing infrastructure will include natural resources control, monetary control, basic precept control, human services, research and development and invention control. The human services agency will provide baby licensing, ID implant processing, education, and health maintenance. The research and development agency will review, approve, and monitor all publicly funded projects that are intended to improve or expand knowledge and know-how in all fields of human endeavor, particularly those that deal with quality of life and enhancement of Earth's ability to support human life. The remaining operational agencies will be discussed in the following chapters.

Thus far in its evolution, humanity has experienced many attempts to unify world politics. The first was the League of Nations and the second was the United Nations that evolved from the League of Nations concept. In addition, there have been many attempts to unify the world under the rule of one political philosophy. The Greeks and Romans come to mind from ancient history. Communism has been a more recent effort to unify the world under one political philosophy.

The intent of Communism is similar to that of the proposed world governing structure. Unfortunately, implementation of the communist concept evolved into a substitute for religion, and its history is similar to that of the Catholic Church. Communist states have tried to impose their doctrine on their people by suppressing individual thought and expression. The results are police states in which personal freedoms are restricted and dissidents are severely punished. The approach didn't work for the Catholic Church and it isn't working for the few countries that are still governed by dictatorial regimes. Look around. All the countries still controlled by Communists or dictators are struggling to survive or they are beginning to move toward a market-driven economy and a more representative, less restrictive form of government.

In a world governing structure based on the basic precept and mutual empathy, individuals will be free to be all they can be and do all they can do as long as what they do and what they become isn't harmful to themselves or to others or to some aspect of Earth's living environment. An agency of the government will manage the economy, but only to the extent needed to ensure that everyone has what he or she needs to sustain himself or herself in a fulfilling existence. Beyond that, the economy will be consumer driven, and commerce will take place in a free enterprise environment that relies on mutual empathy to eliminate practices and processes that violate the basic precept.

Creation of the United Nations was definitely a step in the right direction. In fact, it might even provide the political framework for a world governing structure. The problem is, the United Nations, as it currently exists, is based on a charter that is full of compromises that were necessary to bring together all the nations that had opposed each other during the Second World War and ensuing Cold War. Furthermore, even though the charter addresses human rights, the United Nations has no way of implementing the kind of world infrastructure being discussed in these writings because the distrust between sovereign nations is just as palpable today as it was when the UN began. Not only that, self-serving national leaders are just as paranoid about losing control of their land and its people now as they were then. Therefore, in order for the implementation of a world governing structure to take place, people from all nations must accept that the common interests of humanity are more important than the personal interests of any individual or the special interests of any group of individuals. In others words, individual selfishness and national paranoia must end before a world governing structure can become a reality.

CHAPTER 31

Consolidate Efforts Worldwide to Maintain Law and Order

The basic precept control group will be responsible for encouraging every-one to engage only in behavior and activities that have a positive effect on a person's own well-being as well as the well-being of every other one of Earth's occupants and all aspects of Earth's living environment that will be affected by every action taken. Consequently, a checklist must be developed that every per-son is expected to follow in responding to the different kinds of motivation or provocation experienced throughout a person's lifetime..

In the beginning, everyone would have to be taught how to use the check-list. Afterward, adults would be expected to teach their children. Eventually, all persons would have learned to diligently adhere to the checklist in all that they do and to diligently correct anyone in their presence who deviates from the checklist, whether acquaintance or stranger. Afterward, every human being will be expected to use the same deliberative process moment by moment and day to day to decide whether or not a contemplated action or activity believed to be necessary to make life more enjoyable can be accomplished without harming themselves or any other aspect of creation on Earth. Furthermore, everyone will be expected to be proactive in making sure that everyone else does like-wise. Once everyone begins adhering to these expectations, Earth will become a place where everyone regards everyone else as members of the same community regardless of where on Earth they live.

In order to make this a reality, the congress will have to develop the checklist and establish the consequences of failing to adhere to the checklist. The basic precept control group will have to ensure that all human beings adhere to this checklist and mete out the appropriate retribution when they don't. Interpretation and enforcement begin at the precinct level and consist of the judges, arbitrators, investigators, and peace officers who operate within each precinct. Decisions made and actions taken at the precinct level are subject to review, first by a board of elected officials who supervise groups of precincts then by a board of elected regional officials and finally by a board of national officials.

Contiguous precincts will be grouped into districts that contain a fixed number of precincts, and contiguous districts will be grouped into regions that are made up of a fixed number of districts. Each district and region will be presided over by a director who is nominated by the operational department director and appointed by the congress. These directors will be responsible for reviewing the decisions made by the personnel within their jurisdiction and for evaluating their performance.

When a person's behavior violates the basic precept and that behavior does not endanger human life, if the person agrees to eliminate that kind of behavior in the future, there's no need to involve a peace officer. However, if the violator resumes the behavior that he or she agreed to eliminate, these violations will require intervention by the proper authorities. All violations of the guidelines that endanger human well-being must be reported to a basic precept control officer, everyone who witnessed such violations must be identified, and everyone must be willing to participate in any ensuing investigation and trial by corroborating information given regarding what happened.

When a person witnesses behavior or an activity that violates behavioral guidelines but does not involve violence or the threat of violence, the witness is required to speak up and explain to the violator how what they are doing adversely affects their own well-being or degrades something that is essential to everyone's well-being. This is especially important when the witness knows the violator personally. For example, if you see an acquaintance smoking a cigarette, you should make it a point to say something that forces the smoker to acknowledge that smoking harms not only the smoker's health but also the health of anyone who inhales the exhaled smoke. Quoting statistics helps, as does enlisting other acquaintances to confront the smoker as well.

In other words, people who adhere to the basic precept must do whatever they can to encourage everyone they encounter to live by the basic precept as well. Complimenting someone for doing something that adheres to the basic precept reinforces that behavior. Similarly, suggesting alternatives when someone does something that violates the basic precept encourages the violator to consider the ramifications of their behavior more carefully before acting. In the latter case, this can be accomplished by explaining why the suggested alternatives are more supportive of one's own well-being and the well-being of all other aspects of creation that the undertaken behavior is affecting. Of course, when someone is doing something enjoyable and refuses to acknowledge that the action or activity in question is harmful in any way, stronger measures like those already discussed will have to be employed.

After a list has been made of all actions, activities, and procedures that have been established as having an adverse affect on individuals or on some aspect of Earth's ability to function properly, a period of transition will have to be established for each adverse action, activity, or procedure, and people will be required to cease taking any action or engaging in an activity or procedure on the list at or before the end of the transition period. In addition, a list of acceptable alternatives to each forbidden action, activity, or procedure will have to be provided. In the meantime, penalties for engaging in harmful behavior would have to be developed and published so that anyone who is caught participating in an action, activity, or procedure on the list will know what penalty will be meted out when anyone is caught engaging in a listed behavior after the grace period is over. Finally, for those actions, activities, or procedures that require a withdrawal period, enrollment in the appropriate treatment facility will be required so assistance and supervision can be provided during the time it takes a person to learn to stop taking a forbidden action or engaging in a forbidden activity or procedure.

The following are some examples that demonstrate how these steps will persuade nonviolent violators of the basic precept to stop doing whatever it is that violates the basic precept. Consider laws associated with owning and operating an automobile. Presently, laws almost everywhere require owners of automobiles to have a license that verifies they have the skills to operate an automobile safely and that they understand the rules that regulate the driving of their automobile on public roads. Automobile drivers are also required to carry insurance that will pay for injuries to other people and damage to other property if they are held responsible for causing an accident while driving their automobile.

Owners of gasoline-powered vehicles and all other pollution-producing implements would be expected to make their vehicles and implements as fuel efficient and pollution free as possible. In order to force such owners to comply, limits would be placed on the amount of fuel an owner is allowed to obtain over a set period of time. In addition, the owner would be charged an annual operating tax on each fuel-powered implement or vehicle based on the volume of emissions it is expected to produce annually.

On the other hand, rewards will be offered to people who modify their existing vehicles and implements to reduce harmful emissions and improve fuel efficiency. Furthermore, incentive discounts will be offered to people who trade in vehicles and implements that are not fuel and emissions efficient and replace them with vehicles and implements that meet emissions and fuel-efficiency standards.

Unfortunately, in the beginning, there are going to be people who haven't yet learned to use mutual empathy or to follow the basic precept and choose not to honor the new rules. When that happens, the violator will be required to undergo remedial training that helps the violator understand why what he or she did is a violation of the basic precept and why adherence to the basic precept is essential. For the initial instance that requires remedial training, the violator will have to take a course that explains mutual empathy and the basic precept, shows why the action taken was a violation, and then uses role-playing exercises that teach the violator how to use mutual empathy and the basic precept in all that they do. For a second offense, the violator will be fined and required to retake the mutual empathy and basic precept training as well as the role-playing exercises. For a third and subsequent offenses, the violator will be fined and required to work in a restricted freedom environment. The period of restricted freedom will depend on the time it takes the violator to earn enough to pay the fines he or she has accumulated from previous offences and to repay any expenditures that had to be made to rectify damage caused by the violator's behavior to property and bystanders.

When a person is sentenced to work in a restricted freedom environment, the work assigned will be the most challenging work the inmate is capable of doing and any necessary training will be provided to ensure proficiency. The value of the work the inmate is able to do will be credited to an account, and the accumulated value of the account will be used to determine when the inmates debt to society have been repaid. This program will enable violators to pay their debt to society while receiving all the training they need to become contributing members of society.

Sometimes a person is falsely accused of having violated the basic precept. In such instances, an arbitrator will be asked to investigate and determine if the accusations are valid or not. If the accusations are valid, the accused will be fined an amount equal to the cost of the investigation and he or she will still be required to finish whatever remedial procedures were prescribed. If the accusations are not valid, the accuser or accusers will be fined the cost of the investigation and the complaints will be expunged from the records of the accused. In addition, the accuser or accusers will be considered to have committed a nonviolent violation of the basic precept and charges will be filed accordingly.

If someone commits an act that violates the basic precept and the act involves violence or the threat of violence, witnesses to the act are required to report what they saw to a basic precept control officer, and the officer's job is to receive such reports and investigate them along with any other evidence to verify that a violation of the basic precept has occurred and that it involves violence or the threat of violence. If the basic precept control officer's inquiries indicate that a violation of the basic precept has occurred, but no deaths are involved, both parties to the incident as well as any witnesses will be asked to attend a hearing with an arbitrator, and the arbitrator will use the basic precept control officer's report to question the parties involved in an effort to resolve the problem out of court. If the arbitrator can't resolve the problem, a court hearing involving judge and jury will be scheduled to decide if a violation has occurred and if so, what the penalty should be.

Such court hearings will involve the arbitrator presenting the details of the case to a judge who will question the opposing parties to determine that the arbitrator's facts are accurate. Once the details of the case have been presented, the judge will interpret the law for the members of the jury and instruct them on how they are to proceed in deciding the issues of the case. When the jury has reached a decision, it will report its findings to the judge along with its recommendation concerning penalties, if any are required. The judge will then announce the jury's decision as well as the penalty to be assessed.

If violence results in someone dying, a basic precept control investigator will try to determine whether the death resulted from premeditated actions or was the result of spontaneous events that resulted in an accidental death. If the death was not caused intentionally, the procedure for handling the case would be the same as the one used for handling violent violations that do not result in someone's death. If the investigator believes the death or deaths resulted from intentional actions, the investigator will have the suspect or suspects arrested and will file a report that serves as justification for a thorough investigation into the events that resulted in murder.

If the investigation indicates that a person or more than one person were killed intentionally, the person or persons that the investigator believes are responsible will be arrested and tried for murder, and if they are found guilty, they will be deprived of their freedom and will spend the rest of their life in restricted freedom, during which they will be employed in the kind of work their education and training enables them to do. Initially, the money earned from that work will be used to compensate the family of the person or persons who were killed. The amount of the compensation will be based on the estimated value of the deceased person's unused life expectancy. Afterward, the money earned will be used to compensate the government for the expense associated with housing, clothing, and feeding the individual or individuals who committed the killing or killings. If it turns out that the killer or killers were hired to do the killing by someone or by others who will benefit from the death of the person or persons being killed, the person or persons who hired the killer or killers will be considered to be just as responsible for the resulting deaths as whoever actually did the killing, and the punishment given them would be identical to that given the person or persons they hired to do the killing.

CHAPTER 32

Establish a Worldwide Education System

The educational services control group will be responsible for ensuring that all individuals are continually evaluated for aptitude, curriculum comprehension, talents, and interests to ensure that they pursue the educational path that enables them to realize the most challenging endeavor that their abilities, interests, and ambitions allow. The educational services control group will also oversee a worldwide public school system and will be responsible for ensuring that the curricula being offered is universally consistent and enables every student to match capacity for learning with aptitude for accomplishing tasks associated with the work each student is interested in pursuing.

Public schools will teach the history of humanity from the perspective of its evolution into a cohesive worldwide community of all human beings, but they will not teach national history, regional history, racial heritage, or religion. These subjects must be taught at home, at church, or by private schools as extracurricular studies that must be paid for with scholarships from the institution providing the course, with money the student has earned from a livelihood, or with money obtained from family members, friends, or acquaintances.

All students, whether they are attending public schools or privately funded schools, will be required to take the same exam at the end of each school term to determine their comprehension of the subject matter contained in the public school curriculum. If a student fails any section of the term exam, that student will be required to participate in remedial studies until such time as the student has demonstrated an acceptable level of understanding of the subject matter covered in the section or sections of the exam that were initially failed. If, during this process, testing indicates that a student has a learning disability that impairs comprehension, that student will be placed in special needs education and a curriculum will be designed to help that student develop into the most functional, productive person his or her capabilities will allow.

The public school curriculum will be formulated using the best ideas presently incorporated in the most comprehensive national education systems from around the world. Perhaps the most widely copied system is the British education system because of the pervasive influence Great Britain has had on the countries that were part of the British Empire and continue to be part of the Commonwealth of Nations. But even in those countries, there are unique differences. Former colonialist powers such as Spain, Portugal, and The Netherlands have also left imprints on their colonies, particularly language. However, when countries subjected to colonization become independent, the educational systems the resulting nations implement are typically structured to accommodate the specific needs of their citizens. Consequently, the curriculum put together by the educational services control group will likely be an amalgamation of the best parts of the best current national systems.

The following constitutes a proposed plan for the comprehensive education of all citizens of the world. To begin with, if all human occupants on Earth are going to learn to get along with one another, it stands to reason that all citizens of the world need to be able to communicate in the same language. Therefore, the universal system of public education will teach one language and that language will be used throughout its curriculum. Furthermore, all public business will be conducted using that language. The use of any other language will be restricted to private communications between individuals and between teachers and students who wish to learn another language. In the latter case, all teachers of another language will be required to register with the educational services control group and be certified as being authorized to teach a language other than the one universally required.

All students will be continually evaluated for aptitude, curriculum comprehension, talents, and interests and will be encouraged to follow the educational path that enables them to realize the most challenging endeavor their abilities, interests, and ambitions allow. The educational services control group will be responsible for ensuring that the curricula being offered to every student matches his or her capacity for learning.

The teachers will be paid a professional wage and the facilities will be state-of-the-art. Coverage will extend from kindergarten through college or vocational training. Students will be continually evaluated for aptitude, curriculum comprehension, talents, and interests so that they can be encouraged to follow the educational path that enables them to realize the most challenging endeavor that their abilities, interests, and ambition allow.

Community schools will not teach national history, racial heritage, or religion. These subjects must be taught at home, at church, or by private schools. Of course, any private school would be expected to offer the same curriculum and evaluation services as the community schools do, so courses on national history, racial heritage, and religion would be extracurricular and the cost of these extracurricular courses would have to be paid for by the student or the student's parents using money earned from a livelihood.

CHAPTER 33

Control Utilization of Earth's Natural Resources

In order to make informed decisions about satisfying the needs of all Earth's people, it is essential that the natural resources control group of the worldwide governmental entity control depletion of Earth's nonrenewable natural resources by managing natural resource harvesting, raw material production, and the manufacturing processes needed to convert raw materials into end products. This will enable the natural resources control group to ensure that everyone has what he or she needs to sustain an adequate standard of living throughout his or her life. Furthermore, by maintaining control of the raw materials needed for luxury products, the natural resources control group can ensure that the processors and fabricators that make these products adhere to guidelines for pollution control as well as worker safety and fair wage standards. If they don't, they won't be able to acquire the materials they need to produce their products. Finally, the natural resources control group will be responsible for implementing durability and efficiency standards.

The natural resources control group would own all Earth's land and its natural resources, and that group would control use of Earth's land and its resources to ensure that all human beings on Earth have adequate housing and are able to obtain the wherewithal to sustain themselves in an acceptable standard of living. The objective is for the government to maintain ownership of all natural resources to ensure that everyone is able to get enough of them and the products made from them to maintain an acceptable standard of living.

Natural resources can be categorized according to the end product. Things like air and water or scenic vistas require no manufacturing, but they do require vigilance in ensuring that these resources remain unaffected so that they continue serving their purpose and are available for everyone's use. On the other hand, natural resources that are irreplaceable must be managed in a way that ensures their availability for as long as possible. Therefore, the natural resources control group would be responsible for controlling the use of all natural resources used in the production of finished products and it would be responsible for controlling the way in which air and water are affected by the production and use of finished products.

MANAGE CONVERSION OF NATURAL RESOURCES INTO FINISHED PRODUCTS

End products would be categorized according to the extent that assembly is required to produce a consumer product. Category one includes all products that have no parts as well as the basic parts that are used in the manufacture of category two and category three products as well as the products needed by consumers to make their own food and clothing, build their own houses, and make their own tools including a means of conveyance. These parts and products require the least amount of assembly, if any, and would be the least expensive. All finished parts and products needed to sustain life at the lowest acceptable level of existence would fall into this category.

Category two would include products that shorten the time and effort needed to create food, clothing, housing, and conveyance from category one products. These products would include preassembled components used in the creation of housing and vehicles, food processors, and ready-made clothes in standard designs and colors. It would also include production of components needed to create category three products.

Category three products include finished goods that address consumer preference to buy products that immediately satisfy a functional need, for example, a dwelling, a means of conveyance, or an appliance. In other words, the price of category three products is typically much higher than similar category two products because it reflects not only greater costs of production, but also the effect on price of limited availability.

The natural resources control group would sell category one products to do-it-yourselfers for their use in doing all the things necessary to sustain an adequate lifestyle and protect themselves from the elements. It would also include the basic products it produces and sells to the assemblers who fabricate category two and category three products.

The price paid for category one products is derived by determining the cost to produce these products plus a set percentage of that cost to cover overhead expenses. Note that there is no cost associated with the natural resources that are consumed by the product itself because those natural resources belong to everyone equally.

The price paid by the consumer for products in categories two and three would include a value-added tax that is calculated as a set percentage of the difference between the cost of harvesting the natural resources and producing the raw materials and the price paid by purchasers of a finished product be it category one, two, or three. This value-added tax would be included in determining the price paid by each succeeding processor and by the end user or consumer. Obviously, the more complicated an end product is in terms of the components and processes required to construct it, the higher its production costs and the higher the value-added tax collected by the natural resources control group.

To summarize, the natural resources control group generates its revenue from the fees it charges for managing the process of harvesting natural resources and converting them into useful products and from a value added tax on category two and category three product sales. It uses that revenue to fund its own operations as well as the operations of all the other governmental groups that provide the services that the government offers free of charge. It will also fund such activities as interplanetary exploration, development of more efficient processes for mining, agriculture, and manufacturing, as well as research into ways to improve health and the quality of life.

This agency will also be responsible for making sure that manufacturers make their products as durable and energy efficient as possible. They will do this by setting product-durability and operating-efficiency standards. They will also implement a monitoring system that tracks the life of every manufactured item and tracks end product performance in terms of energy use. A debit system will also be implemented to encourage manufacturers to produce durable goods and end users to properly maintain those goods so they last at least as long as their longevity standard and, if applicable, operate at least as efficiently as their efficiency standard.

Durability and efficiency standards will have to be developed using input from manufacturers and from research scientists and engineers. Obviously, a timeline will have to be established that identifies incremental improvements over reasonable time intervals, but the starting point will be the expected longevity and operating-efficiency standards for products being manufactured at the outset of monitoring.

In order to implement durability and efficiency standards, the only changes that will be necessary will be the development of a monitoring system. The first step will be to assign an identity code to every component of every manufactured product and to develop a way to affix the code to the manufactured component so that the component can be identified and information about its life can be saved as an integral part of the product. The saved information will provide the date when the component was manufactured, the identity of the manufacturer, the date when the component was assembled into an end product, and the identity of the person or persons who performed the assembly.

End products that consist of multiple components and require a source of energy to function will include a microprocessor that will contain an inventory of all components that make up the end product as well as information about when the end-product manufacturing was completed, when it was sold and to whom it was sold, as well as records of all maintenance and a maintenance timetable that is tied to number of hours of use. The microprocessor will also monitor performance of all components so that it may alert the user if any component is detected that is not operating within its optimum range. In addition, the microprocessor will monitor energy use and notify the user if performance is less than what it should be for the amount of energy being used.

When an end product stops working, the natural resources control group must be notified. Upon notification, a representative of the natural resources control group will inspect the product and obtain a download from the product's microprocessor. From this information, the representative will determine why the product failed and how long the product had been in service. If product failure is due to external forces that have nothing to do with the maintenance or the durability of the product and the product processor component has been rendered inoperable due to what happened, the natural resources control group representative will refer the problem to a peace officer for resolution and will provide the peace officer with all the information the representative has obtained.

If the end product stopped working because one or more components stopped working prematurely, and the cause of failure is not due to external causes, the natural resources control group representative will determine from the information provided by the end product microprocessor whether the faulty component or components failed because of manufacturing defect or because of improper maintenance. If premature component failure is due to improper maintenance, the owner of the end product will be given a debit and the owner's record will be checked for previous debits. If there are none, the owner will have to replace the failed component by purchasing a new one using money earned from a livelihood. If there are other debits, the owner will also have to pay a fine equal to the cost of the replaced component multiplied by the number of debits the owner has accumulated. If any of the previous failures involve the same component whose failure is presently under investigation, the end product will be taken from its owner and placed in inventory for distribution to someone else and an entry will be made in the present owner's record that will prevent that person from acquiring a replacement.

If microprocessor records show that proper maintenance was performed, the natural resources control group representative must then determine if the faulty component or components failed because of poor manufacture or because of poor assembly and debit the appropriate party. In addition, the party at fault must replace the failed component and pay for the cost of installation.

At the end of the year, every manufacturer will be audited to see how it has performed. The audit will consist of reviewing records for each product the manufacturer makes to determine if any of those products caused the manufacturer to receive debits, and if so, how many. The objective is to establish the percentage of failures for each product and compare that percentage to the percentage that the natural resources control group has set as being acceptable. If the computed percentage is greater than the acceptable percentage, the manufacturer will be fined and put on probation for the product whose failures are above standard. If manufacturer is already on probation for the manufacture of that product, its license to manufacture the product will be suspended until it can show that modifications have been made to correct whatever was causing the failures to occur.

The natural resources control group will use data collected by a product's integrated microcomputer to determine if an end product's energy efficiency is being maintained. The end product's microprocessor will keep track of energy used during time in use as well as the work that was done over the period of time that elapsed between readouts. When a product is refueled, performance information is downloaded through the fueling apparatus and forwarded to the natural resources control group that compares the received information with the energy-efficiency standard for the end product identified in the data received. If energy used is in line with the energy-efficiency standard, no action is taken. If the energy being used exceeds the energy-efficiency standard, the natural resources control group will notify the end user that the energy efficiency of the identified end product is below standard and proof of maintenance will be required before additional refueling will be allowed. This should never happen because the end product's microprocessor will have already notified the end user of the performance inefficiency via a warning light, and unless the end user intentionally ignores the warning light, the necessary action to correct the problem will have already taken place.

In order to track end-product performance, every end product that uses an external energy source to power its energy-driven parts will have an integrated microcomputer that keeps track of how the product's components are performing and whether the product is using more energy than it should. This computer will also be able to keep both the end user and the natural resources control group apprised of how well the end product is functioning.

The means of transmitting data to the natural resources control group depends on whether the end product relies on power it creates itself using fuel obtained from an external source such as gasoline or on power generated externally and fed to the end product via connection to a remote power generator as is the case with electricity. If fuel is obtained from a reservoir component that is part of the end product, the end product microcomputer will be connected via plug-in cable to the fuel pump when refueling takes place. That enables the fuel pump to download information from the end product's microcomputer. The information downloaded will identify the end product, its owner, the amount of fuel required to fill up the reservoir, the number of hours of operation since the last fill-up, and the amount time the end unit was engaged in work during that time. At the end of the day, the natural resources control group computer would poll all pumps and download all captured information.

When the end product uses electricity for power, the end-product microcomputer will keep track of the amount of electricity being used and continually compare the amount being used to the amount that the end product should be using for the setting at which the end product is operating. When the amount of electricity used over a unit of time is greater than it should be, the end-product microcomputer triggers a warning light that alerts the end user to the fact that it is not functioning properly. In addition, the end-product microcomputer transmits a signal to the natural resources control group computer that alerts it that the end product responsible for sending the alert is not functioning within parameters.

When the natural resources control group computer receives this kind of alert, it immediately sends a notice to the end user giving the person a specific amount of time to have the appliance repaired. The end user must then take the appliance in for repair by an authorized repair person. If the end product is not transportable, the end user will have to schedule an appointment to have an authorized repair person come out and do the necessary repairs on site. Afterward, whether the repairs are done on site or at a repair facility, the repair person will communicate electronically with the natural resources control group to confirm that the repairs have been made and that the warning light has been reset.

If the warning light is not reset by the end of the time allotted to have repairs made, the natural resources control group computer will transmit a signal to the end-product microprocessor that disables it from further use. After that, the only way the owner can continue using it is for the user to pay a fine and also pay for necessary repairs. Of course, the owner may choose to replace the item with a new one in which case, the owner would follow the procedure described previously, namely, trade in the old item for a refurbished or brand new replacement.

A similar kind of system would be used to monitor complex products such as the automobile. The automobile is a perfect example of an end product that contains many components, some of which are made up of multiple components, for example, the engine. Since an automobile is made up of systems and subsystems that are assembled separately and then added as the automobile is being constructed, each of those systems or subsystems would have its own microprocessor and it would monitor that system's or subsystem's performance and signal the automobile's end-product microprocessor when one of the components it monitors is not performing up to standard.

When the end-product microprocessor detects that a component of a subsystem or system is no longer working efficiently, that component is replaced. Using the automobile engine as an example, things such as spark plugs and pumps that are on the periphery can be replaced without having to replace the whole motor. Otherwise, the whole subsystem or system would be replaced and the subsystem or system being replaced would then be disassembled so worn parts can be replaced and the subsystem or system can be reassembled and placed in inventory. In addition, the worn parts would be checked to see if their time in service is at least equal to their longevity standard. If so, they are recycled. If not, they are referred to the natural resources control group for analysis and appropriate action if the malfunction is attributable to faulty manufacturing or installation. When a component's time in use reaches its longevity standard, the microprocessor unit that monitors it will notify the end user and alert the natural resources control group so the procedure discussed earlier can be set in motion.

For end products such as bicycles that have multiple components and need to be properly maintained but are not subject to energy-efficiency monitoring, there will still need to be a way to identify parts by their part code and to determine the manufacturer, the date of manufacture, the date of assembly, and the identification of the person responsible for ensuring that assembly was done properly. If appropriate, the end product will also have a battery-powered microprocessor that monitors sensors on wheel axles to keep track of wheel revolutions and alert the owner when part lubrication or tire maintenance is required.

For these kinds of products, the natural resources control group would get involved only when a part breaks down and a replacement part is needed, the end product owner wishes to replace a part because it has reached its durability standard, or the owner wishes to trade in the end product for an improved version. In the latter case, the natural resources control group would only allow a trade to take place if it is satisfied that the end product being traded in has been properly maintained, is operating efficiently, and cannot be modified to attain the same functionality as the improved version.

MANAGE LAND USE TO ENSURE HUMANITY'S WELLBEING

Since human beings on Earth are expected to share Earth's land and the natural resources it contains or produces equitably, the natural resources control group will need to initiate and coordinate the conversion of land from individual ownership to universal ownership. This conversion will entail inventorying and categorizing land according to it best use, then initiating a program whereby individuals are allowed to bid for the right to occupy or to use a plot of land for its intended purpose (i.e., residential land, farm and ranch land, national park land, commercial land, and public land for things like urban parks, schools, roads, and waterways).

When the world governing entity assumes control, the natural resource control group will assume ownership of all land and its resources, and the land will be inventoried and classified according to its primary intended use. The previous owners of private land will be given the right to continue to occupy the land their residence is on and to work any income-producing land they own when the natural resources control group assumes ownership, if that land is given an income producing classification.

The owner of a right-to-work, income-producing property, in effect, is working for the natural resources control group and is compensated on a cost plus basis that provides the owner of the right with a reasonable return on time and investment. Bonuses will be paid for increased productivity as long as those gains are not made by deferring maintenance on equipment, or by paying labor less than a fair wage. The right to work income-producing land can be bought and sold, and the owner will be able to pass ownership of those rights to heirs, but if the owner abandons an income-producing property or fails to work it properly, the natural resources control group will have the right to take the right back from the derelict owner and either resell it or keep it and hire a contractor to work the property properly.

Rights to residential plots will be given to applicants on a first come, first served basis. The right gives its owner permission to use a specific plot of land as the site for a residence. The right is free but if the plot already has improvements on it, the applicant must pay the natural resources control group for them since that agency will have either had the improvements made or will have reimbursed the previous owner who made them.

Residential land as it existed when the natural resources control group assumed ownership will be replotted so that each plot contains enough area for a dwelling with a foundation area that supports a single-family dwelling adequate enough to accommodate a family of up to four individuals as well as the space needed for a garden and storage for acceptable tools and vehicles. Dwellings needed to accommodate families with more than four members will have to be multistory to avoid requiring a larger foundation.

Some plots will be set up to accommodate high-rise buildings with multiple residences and enough surrounding area to provide garden space and storage for every residential unit in the building. Plots for parks, schools, and governmental services as well as plots for retail and commercial enterprises will be interspersed with residential land. This will allow the services and amenities most people require for day-to-day living to be located within walking distance, and that will help reduce the use of motorized transportation that consumes natural resources and produces pollution.

When someone obtains a plot that has no improvements and the person chooses to build a house himself, he can obtain the necessary materials using a credit balance that each person is given annually (See chapter 35 for more about how the credit balance will be facilitated and used). This enables him or her to acquire the natural resources and things made from natural resources he or she will need to complete the project. This is the same credit balance that people use to acquire the wherewithal to sustain an adequate lifestyle. Equity in their dwelling is created from the effort they expend in putting the house together themselves or from using money from a livelihood to pay someone else to put the house together for them.

When an owner of a residential plot dies, the right to that plot reverts to the natural resources control group, unless it is claimed by a surviving member of the deceased owner's immediate family. If the right is not claimed, the value of the improvements is paid to the estate of the deceased by the natural resources control group and the right to the residential plot is placed back into the inventory of available plots. In the latter case, someone else may then claim the plot, but the person will have to pay for any improvements that have been made using money earned from a livelihood.

When the transition takes place, the owners of existing residences that are larger than the standard housing unit will be allowed to keep their residence. However, the residence must not occupy more land than is allocated to the standard single-family dwelling. Therefore, any excess land will be replotted and put to another use. If the replotted space is sufficient to accommodate a standard housing unit, it may be used for that purpose, but it could also be used as a park, commercial property, or for some other type of community infrastructure.

While the credit balance limits the amount of materials that a new dwelling can contain, the only restrictions on the type of house that one chooses to build will be those imposed by the community in which the house is located. Each community will have a homeowners association that is responsible for establishing any restrictions on a structure's external façade.

No individual or family unit is entitled to own and occupy more than one residential property. Those that own more than one residence when the natural resources control group assumes control will be allowed to choose which residence they wish to retain as their dwelling. All other residential properties will be purchased by the natural resources control group and placed in the inventory of available properties to be distributed on a first-come, first-served basis. In instances where families or individuals have to sell excess residential properties, the natural resources control group will reimburse them for the estimated value of the improvements.

If a reclaimed property has special appeal because of its location or the magnitude of improvements, the natural resources control group may designate the property to be a vacation house that will be made available for rent on a month-to-month basis. In such cases, the previous owner of the property will be not only be reimbursed the value of the property, but also will be given the right to reserve the property for use for a limited period of time annually. The remainder of the time, the property will be available for rent to others on a first-come, first-served basis. Vacation house maintenance and management will be handled by an employee of the natural resources control group who is responsible for a portfolio of such properties that are located in the same community.

Rental property that's owned by an individual, family, or group will be handled much like second homes will be handled. The owners will be reimbursed for the estimated value of the improvements, then the individual units will be put into inventory and made available on a first-come, first-served basis to anyone who wishes to have a former rental unit as his or her residence. In instances where a rental property has multiple units and no one wants any of the units as his or her residence, the property will be converted to other uses or replaced with an improvement that meets the specific needs in the area.

In certain instances, the nature of the units in a rental property may be such that they can be converted to use as permanent accommodations. When this is the case, the renter of a unit that has been taken over by the natural resources control group will be given the opportunity to buy the right to the unit for use as his or her residence. As with other types of residences, the person will have to pay the natural resources control group the estimated value of the improvements, but payment can be made over time and the payments will be the same as the rent the person had been paying.

Properties used in business and industry will continue to be used for whatever purpose they had prior to the transition. As with other types of real estate, ownership of the land will transfer to the natural resources control group, but ownership of the improvements will remain with whomever owned them before, and they will be allowed to continue using them to conduct their business as long as they adhere to guidelines concerning pollution control, product safety, and employee well-being. If absentee owners are involved, they will be reimbursed for the estimated value of the improvements and the natural resources control group will assume management of those improvements in order to maintain a direct relationship between the natural resources control group and the users of the improvements.

CHAPTER 34

Implement Procedures to Protect All Water Resources

Since water is perhaps the most important resource on Earth because of the many ways it is used, its availability is one of the most important factors in sustaining the various kinds of life that exist on Earth. Therefore, the natural resources control group will be responsible for implementing a worldwide system that provides adequate supplies of water to all places on Earth where life exists.

In order to accomplish this objective, all water that exists on Earth will have to be recognized as a commodity in the same way other natural resources are considered commodities. Second, the balance between water as a resource and water as an environment must be maintained. Third, processes for reclaiming water or creating water must be integrated into the system so that water can be made available wherever it's needed, particularly where it's scarce or nonexistent at present.

Water is the living environment for a significant number of the species of life that inhabit Earth. Therefore, the natural resources control group must ensure that sufficient water is reserved to serve that purpose and that it remains in the state that best supports those species that inhabit it. Since almost all the water in the world is contained in Earth's oceans and seas and since that water contains salts and minerals that make its use for human consumption problematic, the water available for human consumption amounts to about 3 percent of all water on Earth, and of that 3 percent, only 30 percent or less than 1 percent is actually available as potable fresh water. The rest is locked up as ice and snow primarily in Antarctica.

In order for the natural resources control group to provide fresh water wherever it is needed to support life on Earth, it must coordinate water reclamation not only from natural fresh water sources such as lakes, streams, underground aquifers, and accumulations of snow and ice in glaciers, but also from salt water using desalination technology and from the atmosphere using fuel-cell technology.

Fuel cells utilize a chemical process that combines oxygen from the air with hydrogen extracted from a hydrocarbon such as natural gas and produces water and electricity as byproducts of the process. The beauty of the fuel-cell process is that it relies on elements that are constantly being produced as part of a natural cycle. Oxygen is put into the air by green plants that use photosynthesis to convert water and carbon dioxide into carbohydrates. Organisms that take in oxygen through their respiratory system expel carbon dioxide. And the carbohydrates that plants produce are a renewable source for the hydrocarbons needed in the fuel cell. Gas produced by properly managed waste dumps are also a source that could be used.

Unfortunately, this process is too costly for common use at the moment because it uses platinum as a catalyst, but research is ongoing, and eventually, fuel-cell technology will become the most cost-effective way to provide potable water and a nonpolluting source of electrical power to places where neither is presently available. It's certainly one option in a universal plan to provide water wherever it's needed.

Water to be used for any purpose would be obtained from the natural resources control group through its distribution system. In other words, water from the oceans, seas, lakes, streams, and underground aquifers would belong to the natural resources control group, and this agency will endeavor to make potable water available everywhere on Earth that habitation is possible. They should be able to do this by utilizing either a pipeline network that distributes water from where it's obtainable to where it's needed or a fuel-cell system that generates water and electricity in places where pipelines are impractical. Where pipeline networks are used, they would function much like the power grids that supply electricity.

The natural resources control group would also be responsible for reclaiming water from sanitary sewage, industrial processes, and agricultural runoff and converting it into water that industry and agriculture can use instead of potable water from lakes, streams, and aquifers. This will minimize depletion of potable water sources better used to support human and other life forms that need potable water in order to survive.

The natural resources control group will assume ownership of all power generating plants and power grids. Acquisition will be handled like other income-producing properties and the previous owners will be encouraged to continue operating the power plants they owned on a cost-plus-incentive basis. Of course, the natural resources control group will require that all power plants that need to be upgraded will be to eliminate pollution violations and that the power grid is operated in a fail-safe, efficient manner.

Electricity will be provided to everyone regardless of where he or she lives, but in places where it's not economically feasible to install a power grid, residents will be provided with a power-generating alternative. Depending on the circumstances, that alternative may be a wind turbine, fuel cells, solar panels, or people-powered generators.

People-powered generators are accomplished by peddling a bicycle-like stationary device so that a fly-wheel generates electricity and stores it in rechargeable batteries. There are already multiple systems on the market that enable people living in the most remote places on Earth to use electric lights, portable computers, and other devices powered by electricity obtained from rechargeable batteries. All that's left is for the natural resources control group to standardize the specifications for the self-operated, power-generating system it will subsidize and make available to those who choose to live where electricity is not otherwise available.

Like everything else, the credit balance can be used to cover the costs of the natural resources contained in such devices, but the remainder of the price for a self-powered electricity generation must be paid for with funds earned from a livelihood. The advantage of generating electricity in this way is that the only limit to the amount of electricity a person can use is the amount of effort that person is willing to put into generating it.

The natural resources control group will establish allotments for the amount of potable water each individual each can use to satisfy his or her physical and hygienic needs. It will also provide allotments of unpotable water for use in the maintenance of the durable products people are permitted to own, the maintenance of grass and plants they are permitted to grow, and for instances where water is used as a coolant to facilitate operation of motorized equipment. This will help save on costs to purify water that will not be consumed by humans to sustain their physical health.

For residents living in places where it is not economically feasible to provide electricity and water, their credit balance can be used to acquire the equipment needed to generate their allotment of electricity and potable water. However, there will still be restrictions on the amount of water that can be extracted from above and underground sources including rainwater collected from roof runoff .

The environmental control group and the natural resources control group will have to work together to prevent nonbeneficial uses of waterway ecosystems from preventing their beneficial uses. For example, sometimes an alien plant species is introduced into a waterway ecosystem for well-intended reasons, but the result is more harmful than beneficial. That was the case when Salt Cedar was introduced along the Pecos River as a decorative plant. Salt Cedar gives off a chemical that kills native plants and it uses inordinate amounts of water. Consequently, this plant began turning vibrant land into waste land because water and vegetation became practically nonexistent.

Sometimes, water plants that benefit water occupants can create detrimental consequences if they are allowed to grow uncontrolled and either reduce sunlight allowed to penetrate the water's surface or clog waterways to the extent that habitat is threatened. In such cases, the environmental control group and the natural resources control group will be responsible for coordinating efforts to ensure that all water is used to benefit all Earth's inhabitants equitably and that as little of it as possible is lost to nonbeneficial purposes.

CHAPTER 35

Establish Equitable Health Maintenance for All Human Beings

Today, it's fairly standard practice in most countries to engage in preventive medicine to interrupt the propagation of communicable diseases that cause debilitation or death. Unfortunately, there are many known diseases for which no cure has been discovered and it is very likely that there are diseases that have not yet manifested sufficiently to be recognized as a threat to human well-being. Therefore, a world health and disease control group must be established to support research into the causes of and cures for human diseases. This group would also be responsible for providing preventive health care solutions to all human beings on Earth.

For the world health and disease control group to accomplish its mandate, it must discover ways to improve humanity's ability to function effectively in every place on Earth where human life can be sustained. In order to do that, it would be helpful to be able to identify people who have survived an epidemic or some other health threat. It would also be helpful to be able to identify individuals whose physiological performance is above average as well as individuals who have a physiological deficiency. Therefore, the world health and disease control group must develop a monitoring system that enables it to continuously record the environmental influences to which every human being is exposed throughout his or her lifetime. In addition, another kind of monitoring system would have to be developed that records every human being's response to the environmental conditions to which he or she is exposed every moment of his or her life.

These two systems are essential in identifying persons whose physiology enables them to respond differently than others to environmental conditions that have an adverse effect on some human beings.

The monitoring system carried by every human being would use a micro-computer and sensors that are implanted in every individual at birth and remain with their host throughout the host's lifetime. The sensors will be placed just under the epidermis in areas of the body most likely to be affected by exter-nal environmental influences. The implanted microcomputer will be located within the body cavity where it can receive and record signals transmitted to it by the sensors. Every twenty-four hours, the microcomputer will be polled by an external computer at which time it will transmit its collected readings to the polling computer then reset and begin the next data collection cycle. The external computer will analyze readings obtained from every individual and will alert operators if any of the data received deviates significantly from that received in previous readouts.

This system provides an ideal way to identify people who have survived an epidemic or some other health threat, because each individual's microcom-puter would not only identify its host, but also would contain valuable informa-tion about that individual's health as well as information about the individual's whereabouts when the data was collected. Therefore, when an epidemic occurs anywhere on Earth, the data provided by each person's microprocessor will ena-ble investigators to determine whether there are survivors who have a common physical characteristic that enabled them to survive when others exposed to the same influence at the same time and place did not.

The microprocessor could also be used to identify individuals whose physiological performance is above average as well as individuals who have a physiological deficiency. This information would be helpful in improving the physiology of every newborn human being and in keeping those with a deficiency from receiving treatments or medicines that would worsen their health instead of improving it.

When an individual dies, the health and performance records for the deceased individual will be downloaded and saved for use in studies that are trying to determine the quality of life experienced in different places on Earth and identify anything extraordinary about that person's life that might be used to improve the lives of future generations. This information is essential in ensuring that future generations live longer, healthier lives. Afterward, the microcom-puter and sensors will be removed from their deceased host and recycled.

To ensure that all human beings' health is good for as long as they live, the world health and disease control group must work with the natural resources control group to ensure that all people can obtain what they need to sustain an acceptable standard of nutrition and that they have adequate shelter, clothing, and the means to acquire at least the accoutrements of a minimally acceptable standard of living. The world health and disease control group will establish what constitutes acceptable nutrition for all age groups and for all groups with unique physical requirements, and it will publish recommended diets that satisfy each group's nutritional needs. In addition, it will identify processed food and food processing techniques that must be avoided because they contribute to obesity or fail to provide nutritional value.

The natural resources control group will ensure that sufficient resources are committed to the production of the kinds of foods the world health and disease control group recommends. In addition, it will prohibit the production of any processed food that is not approved by the world health and disease control group. Furthermore, it will ensure that everyone consumes only the amount of natural resources and the products made from natural resources that are required to sustain an adequate standard of living.

This can all be facilitated by providing every man, woman, and child with an annual credit balance that is downloaded to each individual's implanted microprocessor. This credit balance can be used to acquire the materials and products that have been deemed by the world health and disease control group to be sufficient to maintain the host individual's health and well-being and by the natural resources control group to be sufficient in sustaining the host individual in a viable existence.

Each person's credit balance will enable that person to obtain category one products by paying only for fabrication costs unless or until the credit balance is used up. The credit balance can also be applied to that part of the cost of a category two or category three product that is attributed to the value of the natural resources used in the product. The value added from fabrication and finishing as well as a value-added tax must be paid for with money earned from a livelihood.

Therefore, when a person buys a finished product, he or she will have to pay for the costs associated with harvesting, processing, finishing, distributing, and marketing that product plus the profit margin and the accumulated value-added taxes, but the person won't have to pay for the raw materials used to create the end product because everyone is entitled to their share of Earth's raw materials. However, several points need to be kept in mind. First, the annual credit balance is sufficient to acquire only those things the world health and disease control group has determined are necessary to support one individual in a viable existence for one year. Once the credit balance reaches zero, acquisition of additional goods of any kind will not be permitted. Second, the consumer must pay for the costs associated with creating an end product and for the profit margin and value-added taxes on that product using money earned from a livelihood. Third, durable goods, like clothing, tools, and implements should only have to be purchased once. Larger sizes, different styles, or more effective implements can be obtained by trading in a previously acquired one for a replacement.

Since everyone owns the world's natural resources and is entitled to enough of them to sustain a viable existence, the world health and disease control group will have to determine how much of Earth's natural resources each person is entitled to consume to sustain a viable existence. The amount allocated will be gender and age specific. Then, a credit balance deemed sufficient to sustain each individual for one year will downloaded to the individual's microprocessor. The download will occur on each individual's birthday. Afterward, each time that person acquires something durable that was made from natural resources, his or her credit balance will be adjusted until the balance reaches zero. This system will enable the government to keep track of how much of its allotment each individual has already used and how much is left to get the person through to the end of his or her current allotment period.

The objective of the system is to allow all people to realize their birthrights, and as long as they're satisfied with making their own clothes, building their own houses, and growing their own food, their cost of living will be the sum of the minimal costs they incur to acquire fabricated implements they are not able to make themselves. On the other hand, the system doesn't restrict anyone from pursuing a livelihood that allows them to buy prefabricated products and finished goods rather than having to make everything themselves.

As for the effect this system will have on the world economy, it shouldn't affect it at all as long as the majority of people continue to prefer earning money from a livelihood rather than spending all their time and effort maintaining a subsistence lifestyle. Obviously there will be a reduction in overall demand for products because of limits placed on the amount of natural resources each person can consume, but there will also be a reduction in the costs associated with obtaining raw materials. Therefore, as long as enough people continue to eschew a subsistence lifestyle and prefer working at a job that allows them to earn enough to purchase the things they need to attain a more preferable lifestyle, the industrial complex won't go away. However, it will evolve as more and more people acquiesce to lifestyles influenced by mutual empathy rather than attitudes of entitlement, ego, and self-interest.

Implementing these changes will require the various control groups within the government to work together to ensure that the process by which natural resources are harvested and turned into useful products is sufficient to adequately sustain everyone in a standard lifestyle. It will also help minimize depletion of natural resources and eliminate, or at least minimize, all byproducts that are harmful to some aspect of creation on Earth.

The natural resources control group and the world health and disease control group must also be concerned with how to keep the human population on Earth from reaching unsustainable levels. Consequently, they must introduce a requirement that that every person has the right to replace oneself. In other words, instead of allowing couples to have as many children as they want, they will only be allowed to produce two unless there are extenuating circumstances.

To control the birth rate, all couples wishing to have a child must first obtain a permit to do so. To get a permit, both potential parents will be required to take the classes that provide permit seekers with information about how to handle all aspects of having a child starting with sex education and continuing with proper nurturing techniques and requirements for the child's education. The prospective parents will also be required to undergo testing and evaluation to determine their suitability to be parents. Furthermore, if they've previously had children, past performance records will be reviewed to ensure that their parenting skills are up to standards. The objective of these requirements is to ensure that the permit seekers are capable of providing an emotionally stable environment in which to raise their child so that the child is more likely to receive the nurturing that will help him or her develop into a fully functional, productive individual.

The courses on child care that both parents must take include how to use child psychology properly to ensure that their children will develop the kinds of character traits they'll need to be fully functional members of their community. That means parents must be taught a way of interacting with their children that may differ from the way they were treated by their parents or whoever raised them. In order to do that, everyone will have to be trained on how to apply the basic precept when interacting with his or her children as well as with everyone else, for that matter.

Since every child is entitled to the opportunity to develop into a fully functioning adult who is able to contribute his or her unique capabilities to improving the quality of human existence, prospective parents must be required to take classes that teach them how interactive behavior with their child and with each other affects their child's development. These classes are essential because they teach parents the importance of modeling behavior influenced by mutual empathy and the basic precept in order to influence their children to do the same.

Requiring couples wishing to have a child to obtain a permit will not only help control population growth, but will also improve the chances that every child who is born will enjoy a full and rewarding life. The problem facing the government is how to persuade people to accept this limitation on their freedom to do as they please. The answer is incentives. Those couples who get a permit to have a baby get free education, free childcare, free aptitude evaluation, and free health care for the baby both before and after the baby is born. If a couple does not get a permit before having a baby, that baby will be taken away from its biological parents at birth and given to a couple that has obtained a permit to have a baby, but has not been able to conceive one.

In addition, birth records will be checked to determine if either of the biological parents involved has caused another baby to be born without first obtaining a permit. If not, both will be warned that failure to obtain a permit before having another baby will result in sterilization of the repeat offender. If either or both have already been warned, they will be sterilized.

Under this program, every couple is entitled to have two children. However, there are always going to be individuals who do not want or are unable to have children, and there will be those who reach sexual maturity but die before they can reproduce. So, if a couple who already has two children wants more, they will be allowed to do so if they satisfy all the requirements for obtaining a permit and there is a worldwide deficit in the number of children being produced by their generation.

On the other hand, not being able to have children doesn't mean that a person's contribution to genetically improving the human species will be lost. As discussed previously, a monitoring system can be used to ensure that all DNA responsible for improving human body characteristics is identified and then introduced into all subsequent embryos that need it so the natural selection process can be accelerated.

CHAPTER 36

Establish Worldwide Management of Economic Activity

In order to have a more effective worldwide economy, it will be necessary to convert all the currencies presently in existence on Earth to a universally accepted currency that will be used exclusively throughout the world. The most stable national currency in existence at the time of transition will be used as the benchmark for the new world currency. The exchange rate for that currency to the world currency will be one for one. The exchange rate for all other national currencies will be the same as the exchange rate that each nation's currency has to the benchmark currency at the time the switch-over takes place.

The world community governing entity will include an economic control group that is in charge of maintaining stability in financial matters. It will oversee banks, monitor interest rates, regulate the volume of currency in circulation, and manage economic activity worldwide. It will also act as the government's treasurer taking in the monies that the government receives from the sale of natural resources, the sale of land improvements, and the taxes paid by consumers on the purchases they make. It will disburse funds to the various governmental agencies for operating expenses and to individuals for land improvements when their property is reclaimed by the government.

In order to manage the world's economy, the economic control group will maintain a model that predicts the demand for products, and it will use that model to determine how much and what kind of natural resources are needed to meet that demand. The first priority for resource allocation would be to ensure that the basic needs of the do-it-yourselfers are satisfied. Then and only then would resources be allocated to the production of items most people would prefer to buy rather than make themselves. Finally, if demand warrants it, essential goods utilizing finer finished materials will be offered for sale to those whose livelihood enables them to pay for the higher cost of producing these items.

The economic control group will get the data for its worldwide economic model by implementing a data collection system. The system will utilize the implanted microcomputer that every person alive will receive before transition takes place and that everyone born afterward will receive immediately after birth. For this application, the microcomputer will track product purchases the host makes or are made on his or her behalf.

Since the information collected about every economic transaction an individual initiates is captured in their microcomputer's database, profiles can be developed about the basic needs and spending habits for all age groups within each of a range of economic levels within various demographic classifications. This information will enable the natural resources control group to anticipate the need to produce additional goods and determine the number, type, and distribution of the processors and fabricators required to produce them as well as the land needed for harvesting the necessary raw materials. It would also enable all control groups within the government to anticipate the needs of all human beings as population growth patterns around the Earth change. This will enable the government to provide all necessary services to Earth's occupants effectively in terms of timing and expense.

CHAPTER 37

Establish Worldwide Control of Invention

W hen inventors come up with ideas for new products, they will present their ideas to the invention control group, and the invention control group will work with all the other control groups that will be affected by a proposed invention to determine whether the proposed product fills a need not already being filled by another product or improves the effectiveness of a product already in production. If the proposed product meets these criteria, then the appropriate control groups will test market the proposed product and get feedback from potential consumers regarding the proposed product's appeal and usefulness.

For products that appear to have appeal and provide an improvement in usefulness, the appropriate control group will then be allowed to announce that a new invention is under consideration. Details about the improvements the proposed invention will provide will also be presented. If enough orders are forthcoming, the natural resources control group will enter into a contract with a manufacturer to manufacture the number of units needed to supply the initial demand. Once the initial supply of a product has been sold, the invention control agency will analyze the results to determine whether continuing demand justifies starting the cycle over again, first by incorporating potential improvements then test marketing, taking orders, and ultimately producing the next generation of the product.

Thomas Edison is a good example of someone with the mental capability to invent practical products that use electricity to improve the quality of people's lives. Since then, other inventors have continued to conceive new ways to utilize electricity in ever more sophisticated applications. Obviously, ways to utilize electricity is only one example of how a single invention can initiate a cascade of other inventions. There have also been and continue to be ongoing cascades of inventions that improve the effectiveness and efficiency of tools that someone else invented in an effort to make life easier.

It all began when prehistoric people created simple tools to make obtaining their sustenance and protecting themselves from the elements and predators easier and more effective. Eventually they developed easier ways to get from place to place without having to walk. Then, as less time and energy were needed to defend, feed, cloth, shelter, and transport themselves, people began thinking up various ways to help make living life even easier and more enjoyable. In other words, there has been a continuous cascade of inventions as inventors continue trying to improve on an original invention or they think up new ones. For example, manually operated adding machines gave way to electronic adding machines that gave way to electronic computers.

The focus of all these inventions has been, for the most part, on making some aspect of daily living easier and more enjoyable. As tools and the other accoutrements of living became more sophisticated, little attention was paid to how the manufacture and use of all these products would affect Earth's ability to sustain life. Now scientists are beginning to realize that there are limits to Earth's resources and to the amount of pollution it can absorb without degrading its ability to provide an adequate living environment. Consequently, humanity is faced with having to accept that attitudes regarding how we use things to accomplish desired lifestyles have to change so Earth will be able to continue providing an adequate living environment and the natural resources we require to sustain ourselves adequately, never mind opulently.

Today, at least some inventors and consumers are beginning to be more deliberate in considering the effect on Earth's environment and its organisms that a contemplated invention may have. As a result, products and procedures known to have undesirable side effects are being eliminated. Unfortunately, the majority of Earth's human beings have not reached the level of awareness or commitment required to eliminate all inventions that are harmful to some aspect of life on Earth. Therefore, it is necessary for an invention control group of a worldwide governing entity to be responsible for developing universal standards regarding the invention of products and operating procedures to ensure that the direct and indirect effects produced affect Earth's ability to support life as little as possible. Furthermore, this agency will be required to work with all other control groups to ensure consistency in the adherence to these standards by everyone.

When inventors come up with an idea for an invention, they must submit their idea to the invention control group, and the invention control group will determine whether the proposed invention satisfies a justifiable need. If they find that it does, they will then determine whether the proposed invention conforms to the aforementioned standards. If the conclusion to both investigations indicates that development of the proposed invention is a good idea, the invention control group will work with the other control groups to determine whether the proposed invention has a large enough or important enough application to justify further development and production. This procedure is designed to force inventors to do their due diligence and only invent products that satisfy a legitimate need not being satisfied by any other product. It will also force inventors to design products that can be made using nonpolluting processes and whose operation creates as little pollution as possible both during its use and after its usefulness has ended and it is recycled so its reusable materials can be put to other uses.

Epilogue

The objective of this book has been to stimulate creative thinking about how each human being can help make Earth a better place on which to live. Hopefully, some of the suggestions offered will hasten the arrival of a time when all human beings are considered precious and treated equitably. If you care about anyone living on Earth, including yourself, you should take the time to consider what's been discussed here and act accordingly. It will be worth the effort because you will help make Earth a better place to live both now and in the future.